Everyday
JAPANESE

A Basic Introduction to
The Japanese Language & Culture

by Edward A. Schwarz
& Reiko Ezawa

PASSPORT BOOKS
a division of *NTC Publishing Group*
Lincolnwood, Illinois USA

For Christina Kyoko

1991 Printing

This edition first published in 1985 by Passport Books,
a division of NTC Publishing Group, 4255 West Touhy
Avenue, Lincolnwood (Chicago), Illinois 60646-1975 U.S.A.
Originally published by Shufunotomo Co., Ltd., Tokyo, Japan.
Copyright ©Edward A. Schwarz and Reiko Ezawa. All rights
reserved. No part of this book may be reproduced, stored
in a retrieval system, or transmitted in any form, or by
any means, electronic, mechanical, photocopying or otherwise,
without the prior permission of NTC Publishing Group.
Manufactured in the United States of America.

1 2 3 4 5 6 7 8 9 ML 19 18 17 16 15 14 13 12 11 10

TABLE OF CONTENTS

PREFACE

What is **Bunraku? Gagaku? Sumō?** What is a **mikoshi?** A **hanamichi?** A **dohyō?** If you are not sure, you should be—if you want to know Japan. For the things these words (and many others like them) name are so uniquely Japanese that they are untranslatable. Indeed, Western travelers, students, teachers, and businessmen and women in Japan will regularly use these terms even when speaking in their native languages.

Those not familiar with Japan, however, find verbal translations and explanations inadequate to make these terms clear and understandable. It is the realization that words are not enough that inspired us to put this book together. We have attempted to *illustrate* such unique Japanese terms in the belief that one picture is worth a thousand words of explanation. Although we have been unable to illustrate every word in this book, we have illustrated or pictured as many as space allowed. For instance, what is a **mikoshi?** Even if we say that it is a "portable shrine," you cannot fully understand what it is until you can visualize it. Therefore, we have included illustrations of a **mikoshi** so that you will be able to identify it when you see it. Conversely, if you see a **mikoshi** first, you can consult the illustrations of this book to learn what it is called in Japanese.

However, *Everyday Japanese* is more than an illustrated dictionary of Japanese terms. It is also a phrase book of useful Japanese for Westerners. We know that many travelers to Japan will want to communicate with the Japanese in Japanese, since this is an excellent way to learn about Japan. Therefore, we have assembled numerous Japanese expressions and dialogs to make communication as easy and painless as possible.

But this book is still more than an illustrated dictionary of Japanese and a phrase book. It is also an introduction to Japan—primarily through the Japanese language and illustrations, but also through notes that explain certain words and give practical information useful for visitors to

Japan. For instance, the note about **minshuku** (family inn, p. 30) not only describes what a **minshuku** is, but also explains how reservations may be made. Other items we have included are postal rates for international mail (p. 51), banking services (p. 56), and introductions to many Japanese arts, sports, religions, and other things Japanese (especially in Part Two, "Only in Japan"). While there may be many books available on Japanese art, sports, and religion, we hope that our introductory approach will provide enough information and vocabulary for you to be able to pursue your interests in Japan intelligently.

In preparing this book, we had many different kinds of readers in mind. For tourists, we have tried to provide language aids that will help them have a pleasant trip in Japan. For tourists who find Japanese pronunciation difficult, we have included Japanese written characters for every word, phrase, and sentence, so that they may communicate by showing this book to Japanese and letting them read the appropriate phrases or sentences for themselves. We also hope that tourists will also find this book an informative introduction to many things Japanese, from food to the arts.

For those who plan lengthy stays in Japan, we have included Part Three, "Living in Japan," which deals with such important business as immigration and the buying or renting of a house or an apartment. We also hope that this book will be a handy reference work for such everyday needs as postal rates for international mail and for words which are easily forgotten.

For the serious student of the Japanese language, we hope that the inclusion of **kanji** (Chinese characters) and **hiragana** (the Japanese syllabary) will be helpful.

We also hope that the vocabulary will be a useful supplement to the word lists normally found in Japanese-language textbooks.

Finally, we must say a word about learning Japanese and about this book. We don't want to disappoint you, but this book will not teach you to speak Japanese like a native. Many books claim, or imply, that they can teach you Japanese instantly, or at least in ten easy lessons. Well...it just isn't possible. And we do not make such claims. You will not be fluent in Japanese even if you learn everything in this book. In fact, we have not even attempted to arrange the sections of the book in order of increasing difficulty, as a good textbook would. Rather, we have arranged the sections according to common situations and included the most useful Japanese for each section. Above all, we hope that *Everyday Japanese* will be an effective and enjoyable way for you to meet Japan by becoming acquainted with its language and culture.

E.A.S., R.E.

ACKNOWLEDGMENTS

It is impossible for us to express adequately our gratitude for the assistance and encouragement which many persons have given us in the preparation of this book. However, we would like to mention at least a few of the people who have helped us so much. First, we want to acknowledge a special debt to our good friend and best critic, Thomas Reibner, for his numerous suggestions and valuable advice.

For his recommendations and for his continued instruction about Japan and especially about Japanese music, we wish to thank Professor Kuzan Takahashi, master of the *shakuhachi* and of life. We also want to express our sincere gratitude to Yuzo Fujiyoshi for his timely encouragement and very helpful counsel.

Another person we want to thank is Masahiro Suda of Associate An, Ltd., who gave freely of his expert technical and photographical talents. And we cannot forget the careful and difficult work of Toshiaki Ono, who provided us with the main illustrations for this book.

We owe a special debt of gratitude to Yoshihisa Oshida, president of the Japan Gagaku Society, for his personal pictures of *gagaku, bugaku, kagura,* and the *hichiriki* player, not to mention his generous assistance in helping us better understand *gagaku* and obtain other pictures.

We also want to acknowledge the work *Shōzoku-Zufu* from the series *Kojitsu-Sōsho* as the source for our pictures of *sokutai* and *jūnihitoe,* reprinted here by permission.

For the many pictures provided by the gracious people of the Japan National Tourist Organization (marked throughout the book as JNTO), we wish to express our deep thanks. And for other pictures we want to thank the very busy but helpful people of the Toei Movie Company.

Last, but not least, we wish to thank Kazuhiko Nagai of the International Department of Shufunotomo Co., Ltd., for the original idea that inspired this book, and for his continued advice, assistance, and patience during the preparation of this book.

E.A.S., R.E.

THE ARRANGEMENT OF THIS BOOK

There are three parts in this book. Part One, "Getting Around in Japan," is made up of sixteen common situations in which we have placed main emphasis on words, phrases, and sentences necessary and useful for getting around in Japan. Part Two, "Only in Japan," contains thirteen sections of things which can be found only in Japan, so notes are plentiful while useful expressions and dialogs are kept to a minimum. Part Three, "Living in Japan," is made up of five less common but very useful situations for the person who lives, or decides to live, in Japan. However, we have found it impossible to make each part completely separate from the other two; that is, there is considerable overlap and features of all three parts should be useful for everyone.

Each section of the book contains (1) an illustration and (2) a vocabulary list of twenty words. Subsequent pages of each section contain useful expressions and dialogs (especially in Part One), notes (especially in Part Two), additional words, and/or other features such as pictures or charts of useful information.

Plurals:

English translations for most nouns in this book have been put in the singular, although they could have as easily been put in the plural. Most Japanese nouns do not make a distinction between the singular and the plural. For instance, **hon** means both "book" and "books," although we have listed only the singular form.

SYMBOLS USED IN THIS BOOK

Asterisk: *

An asterisk after an entry of the vocabulary list of twenty words (facing the illustrations) indicates that an explanatory note will be found on one of the subsequent pages of that section.

Brackets: [ ]

Brackets have been placed around words and numbers for which other words and numbers may be substituted. For example, "Chūō" (or the name of any other train line) may replace "Yamanote" as follows:

    [Yamanote]-sen   ([Yamanote] line)
    [Chūō]-sen   ([Chūō] line)

Similarly, "two" may be substituted for "one" as indicated by the brackets:

    [ichi]-bansen   (track number [one])
    [ni]-bansen   (track number [two])

Prefix: (o-), (o)

The prefix *o* is enclosed in parentheses in this book to indicate that it is a term of politeness rather than a part of the word itself. For instance, **mizu** is the common word for "water," but **omizu** is a more polite way of saying the same thing and is written **(o)mizu** for the sake of clarity. In the index of this book, words are listed without the polite prefix **o**.

Suffix: (-san)

In this book, the suffix **-san** is enclosed in parentheses to indicate that it is a term of politeness or address and not a necessary part of the word to which it is attached. For example, **untenshu** means "driver" or "drivers" in general, but **untenshu-san** is used in reference to a particular driver or when addressing him directly (Mr. Driver).

Parentheses: (( ))

Parentheses inside of parentheses are used in certain

English translations to indicate words added for clarity of meaning, although they do not actually appear in the Japanese expression or sentence. For example:

Sumimasen ga.

(Excuse me but. . . (I have a request).)

The added phrase (I have a request) would be understood by both the speaker and the listener of Japanese because the situation (stopping someone on the street to ask directions, for instance) would make the meaning clear.

Abbreviation:　　Lit:

The abbreviation "Lit:" is used to indicate that a subsequent translation is a "literal" one. For example:

Ogenki desu ka?

(How are you? Lit: Are you healthy?)

"Are you healthy?" is a literal translation of the Japanese question which is used in situations when English-speaking people would say "How are you?"

Hyphen:　　　–

Hyphens are included between syllables of words in the basic vocabulary list as an aid to pronunciation. In other places, the hyphens have been dropped due to lack of space except in some places where they add clarity, such as between numbers and counters:

ichi-mai	one thin, flat object
ni-mai	two thin, flat objects

JAPANESE PRONUNCIATION

The Syllabary:

In the Japanese language, each syllable consists of a vowel, or of a vowel and a consonant, except for the syllabic *n* and the letters *k*, *p*, *t*, and *s* when they occur as the first letter of a double consonant. In pronouncing Japanese, each syllable receives approximately equal stress and time. Below is a chart of the Japanese syllables with their **hiragana** (H) and **katakana** (K) systems of writing. **Hiragana** is used in writing Japanese when Chinese characters are not available, and **katakana** is used for foreign words brought into Japanese or for emphasis.

	H	K		H	K		H	K		H	K
a	あ	ア	ka	か	カ	ga	が	ガ	sa	さ	サ
i	い	イ	ki	き	キ	gi	ぎ	ギ	shi	し	シ
u	う	ウ	ku	く	ク	gu	ぐ	グ	su	す	ス
e	え	エ	ke	け	ケ	ge	げ	ゲ	se	せ	セ
o	お	オ	ko	こ	コ	go	ご	ゴ	so	そ	ソ
			kya	きゃ	キャ	gya	ぎゃ	ギャ	sha	しゃ	シャ
			kyu	きゅ	キュ	gyu	ぎゅ	ギュ	shu	しゅ	シュ
			kyo	きょ	キョ	gyo	ぎょ	ギョ	sho	しょ	ショ

	H	K		H	K		H	K		H	K
za	ざ	ザ	ta	た	タ	da	だ	ダ	na	な	ナ
ji	じ	ジ	chi	ち	チ	ji	ぢ	ヂ	ni	に	ニ
zu	ず	ズ	tsu	つ	ツ	zu	づ	ヅ	nu	ぬ	ヌ
ze	ぜ	ゼ	te	て	テ	de	で	デ	ne	ね	ネ
zo	ぞ	ゾ	to	と	ト	do	ど	ド	no	の	ノ
ja	じゃ	ジャ	cha	ちゃ	チャ				nya	にゃ	ニャ
ju	じゅ	ジュ	chu	ちゅ	チュ				nyu	にゅ	ニュ
jo	じょ	ジョ	cho	ちょ	チョ				nyo	にょ	ニョ

	H	K		H	K		H	K		H	K
ha	は	ハ	pa	ぱ	パ	ba	ば	バ	ma	ま	マ
hi	ひ	ヒ	pi	ぴ	ピ	bi	び	ビ	mi	み	ミ
fu	ふ	フ	pu	ぷ	プ	bu	ぶ	ブ	mu	む	ム
he	へ	ヘ	pe	ぺ	ペ	be	べ	ベ	me	め	メ
ho	ほ	ホ	po	ぽ	ポ	bo	ぼ	ボ	mo	も	モ
hya	ひゃ	ヒャ	pya	ぴゃ	ピャ	bya	びゃ	ビャ	mya	みゃ	ミャ
hyu	ひゅ	ヒュ	pyu	ぴゅ	ピュ	byu	びゅ	ビュ	myu	みゅ	ミュ
hyo	ひょ	ヒョ	pyo	ぴょ	ピョ	byo	びょ	ビョ	myo	みょ	ミョ

	H	K		H	K		H	K		H	K
ya	や	ヤ	ra	ら	ラ	wa	わ	ワ	n	ん	ン
			ri	り	リ						
yu	ゆ	ユ	ru	る	ル						
			re	れ	レ						
yo	よ	ヨ	ro	ろ	ロ						
			rya	りゃ	リャ						
			ryu	りゅ	リュ						
			ryo	りょ	リョ						

Vowels:

There are only five vowel sounds in Japanese:

a	sounds like "ah"	as the *a* in father
		(not the *a* in cat or late)
i	sounds like "ee"	as the *i* in machine
		(not the *i* in sit or light)
u	sounds like "oo"	as the *u* in flu
		(not the *u* in cut or cute)
e	sounds like "eh"	as the *e* in get or let
		(not the *e* in me or free)
o	sounds like "oh"	as the *o* in open or hope
		(not the *o* in hot)

Long Vowels:

Long vowel sounds are very important in the pronunciation of Japanese since the meaning of some words will change according to the length of the vowel. For example, **o-ba-sa-n** (aunt) and **o-ba-a-sa-n** or **o-bā-sa-n** (grandmother) are distinguished by the length of the vowel *a*. Japanese write the long vowels in two separate syllables (when using **hiragana**) and if you think of them in the same way it makes pronunciation easier. We have used the following system to indicate long vowels:

ā   (which is the same as **a-a**)
i-i   (since printing a long mark over an *i* is difficult)
ū   (which is the same as **u-u**).
ē   (which is the same as **e-e**)
ō   (which is the same as **o-o**)

In this book, we have consistently indicated long vowels in every word that has them, whether the word appears in a Japanese sentence or an English sentence, with one exception. The exception is that we have not marked long vowels in certain place names which commonly appear in English without long vowel marks, such as Tokyo and Kyoto (**Tōkyō** and **Kyōto** in Japanese).

Short Vowels:

The vowels *u* and *i* are sometimes short; that is, they are not voiced or not pronounced at all when they appear between unvoiced consonants (**f, h, k, p, s, t, ch, sh**) or when *u* appears at the end of a sentence after an unvoiced consonant. Examples:

u between two unvoiced consonants:

su:

	desu ka?	(is it?)	sounds like **deska**?
	sukoshi	(a little)	sounds like **skoshi**
	suki	(like)	sounds like **ski**
ku:			
	kushami	(sneeze)	sounds like **kshami**
tsu:			
	tsukue	(desk)	sounds like **tskue**

fu:

    futatsu   (two)   sounds like **ftatsu**

i between two unvoiced consonants:

shi:

    shite   (doing)   sounds like **shte**

chi:

    chikai   (near)   sounds like **chkai**

ki:

    kitte   (stamp)   sounds like **ktte**
    kippu   (ticket)   sounds like **kppu**

hi:

    hitori   (one person) sounds like **htori**

u at the end of a sentence:

Hon desu. (It is a book.) sounds like **Hon des.**

Consonants:

Most Japanese consonants are pronounced almost the same as English consonants except for the following:

f   is made by blowing air between the lips, without letting the lower lip touch the teeth. The sound produced is approximately halfway between the *h* sound and the *f* sound of English.

g   is hard, like the *g* in go or get (not the *g* in gentle or judge).

n   is sometimes considered to be a full syllable itself (without any vowel). The pronunciation of the syllabic *n* is nasal; that is, the tongue does not touch any part of the roof of the mouth, and air is allowed to escape through the nose. It sounds something like the *ng* in singer or ping-pong, but without the slightest hint of a *g* sound.

    Be careful not to confuse the syllabic *n* with the *n* in **na, ni, nu,** etc. The latter *n* is pronounced the same as the English *n*. When a syllabic *n* is followed by a vowel or *y*, we have separated them with a hyphen or with an apostrophe (**n-a** or **n'a;**

n-yo or **n'yo**).

r   is pronounced between the *l* and *d* sounds of English. It is a flap-r, in which the tip of the tongue momentarily touches the roof of the mouth just behind the teeth.

ch is pronounced like the *ch* in cherry (not like the *ch* in chauvinist or chemistry).

ts is pronounced like the final *ts* in nuts or cuts.

Double Consonants:

kk is pronounced like the *kk* in bookkeeper. The first *k* is a momentary pause (silence) equivalent in time to the pronunciation of one syllable of Japanese; the second *k* is pronounced as usual.

pp is pronounced like the *p* sounds connecting two words in English such as "flip past" (not like the *pp* in a single word such as pepper). The first *p* is a momentary pause (silence) equivalent in time to the pronunciation of one syllable of Japanese; the second *p* is pronounced as usual.

tt is pronounced like the *t* sounds connecting two words in English such as "flight time" (not like the *tt* in a single word such as butter). The first *t* is a momentary pause (silence) equivalent in time to the pronunciation of one syllable of Japanese; the second *t* is pronounced as usual.

tch is a variation of the *tt* sound since the pronunciation of *ch* in Japanese begins with the *t* sound. Therefore, the *t* of *tch* is a momentary pause (like the first *t* of the double consonant *tt*), and the *ch* is pronounced as usual.

ss is pronounced like the *s* sounds connecting two words in English such as "less shame" or "let's sing" (not like the *ss* in a single word such as lesson or less). The first *s* sound is held for the length of time it takes to pronounce one syllable of Japanese, and then the sound is continued into the second *s*.

Part One

Getting Around in Japan

1 General Conversation and Introductions

❶ wa-ta-ku-shi (I)*
わたくし／私

② **a-na-ta (you)***
あなた

③ **ka-re (he)***
かれ／彼

④ **ka-no-jo (she)***
かのじょ／彼女

⑤ **(o-)na-ma-e (name)**
（お）なまえ／（お）名前

⑥ **-sa-n (Mr., Miss, Mrs., Ms.)***
—さん

⑦ **Ni-ho-n-go (Japanese language)***
にほんご／日本語

⑧ **Ni-ho-n-ji-n (Japanese person)***
にほんじん／日本人

⑨ **E-i-go (English language)**
えいご／英語

⑩ **I-gi-ri-su-ji-n (Englishman)**
イギリス人

⑪ **shu-ji-n (my husband)**
しゅじん／主人

❷ **go-shu-ji-n (other's husband)**
ごしゅじん／ご主人

❸ **ka-na-i (my wife)**
かない／家内

❹ **o-ku-sa-n (other's wife)**
おくさん／奥さん

❺ **o-bā-sa-n (grandmother)**
おばあさん

❻ **o-ji-i-sa-n (grandfather)**
おじいさん

❼ **mu-su-ko (my son)**
むすこ／息子

❽ **o-jō-sa-n (other's daughter)**
おじょうさん／お嬢さん

❾ **i-mō-to-sa-n (other's younger sister)**
いもうとさん／妹さん

❿ **(o-)to-mo-da-chi (friend)**
（お）ともだち／（お）友達

3

NOTES:

*❶ **watakushi**: Newcomers to Japan are generally encouraged to use the term *watakushi*, but it is helpful to know that other terms meaning "I" are used by the Japanese depending upon sex and social relationships. For example, men often use the term **boku** (I 僕) when speaking in informal situations. Women may use the more feminine **watashi** (I 私), although *watakushi* is also commonly used. However, these and other terms for "I" are used much less frequently in Japanese than in English, since context often makes them redundant. (In an attempt to make the dialogs in this book consistent with Japanese usage, we have refrained from using the terms *watakushi* or *anata* although the English translation requires the terms *I* or *you*.) Plural: **watakushitachi** (we, 私たち).

*❷ **anata**: There are also many terms for "you" in Japanese. *Anata* is the more formal term, used by both men and women, but men will use **kimi** (you, 君) or **omae** (you, おまえ) in informal situations. Used much less frequently than "you" in English, terms for "you" in Japanese can sound strange if spoken too often. Plural: **anatagata** (you, あなたがた).

*❸ **kare**: This term is not commonly used except informally, as in reference to male friends or acquaintances. The term *kare* is not equivalent to the English term "he" and should be used sparingly.

*❹ **kanojo**: *Kanojo* is used in informal situations to refer to female friends or acquaintances. As with the term *kare* (above), *kanojo* is not exactly equivalent to the English term "she" and should be used sparingly.

*❺ **-san**: This should always be used when addressing someone else. Never use *-san* when speaking about yourself. This term has several alternates which are used to show relationships between people. The term **-sama** (Mr., Miss, Mrs., Ms. -様) is a polite form which elevates the person addressed (and which is used in addressing letters). Sometimes the term **-kun** (-君) is used instead of *-san* when someone speaks familiarly with men younger than, or subordinate to, himself. The term **-chan** (-ちゃん) is an expression of endearment, most often used with children. All of these terms are placed after a person's name (e.g. Jones-san, Tanaka-sama). The term **sensei** (teacher, doctor 先生) literally means "born before" but is used as a term of respect with any instructor, formal or informal. *Sensei* may be used with or without the person's name preceding it.

*❼ **Nihongo:** *Nihon* means Japan, and the suffix *-go* means language; together they mean the Japanese language. Similarly:

Furansu	(France)	フランス
Furansugo	(French)	フランス語
Doitsu	(Germany)	ドイツ
Doitsugo	(German)	ドイツ語
Chūgoku	(China)	中国
Chūgokugo	(Chinese)	中国語

*❽ **Nihonjin:** In this case, *-jin* is a suffix meaning people. Other examples:

Amerika	(America)	アメリカ
Amerikajin	(American)	アメリカ人
Indo	(India)	インド
Indojin	(Indian)	インド人
Itaria	(Italy)	イタリア
Itariajin	(Italian)	イタリア人
Kanada	(Canada)	カナダ
Kanadajin	(Canadians)	カナダ人

ADDITIONAL WORDS:

bokokugo (mother tongue, native language 母国語)
akachan, akanbō (infant, baby 赤ちゃん，赤ん坊)
kodomo, okosan (child 子供，お子さん)
kyōdai (brothers and sisters 兄弟，姉妹)

RELATIONS: The Japanese language provides a clear distinction between my relatives and yours (or another's relatives), as can be seen from the following:

	My		Your; Other's	
haha	母	(mother)	okāsan	お母さん
chichi	父	(father)	otōsan	お父さん
musuko	息子	(son)	musukosan botchan	息子さん ぼっちゃん
musume	娘	(daughter)	musumesan ojōsan	娘さん お嬢さん
ane	姉	(older sister)	onēsan	お姉さん
ani	兄	(older brother)	oniisan	お兄さん
otōto	弟	(younger brother)	otōtosan	弟さん
imōto	妹	(younger sister)	imōtosan	妹さん
sofu	祖父	(grandfather)	ojiisan	お祖父さん
sobo	祖母	(grandmother)	obāsan	お祖母さん
oji	伯父 叔父	(uncle)	ojisan	伯父さん 叔父さん
oba	伯母 叔母	(aunt)	obasan	伯母さん 叔母さん
mago	孫	(grandchild)	omagosan	お孫さん
oi	おい	(nephew)	oigosan	おいごさん
mei	姪	(niece)	meigosan	姪御さん
itoko	いとこ	(cousin)	oitokosan	おいとこさん

6

USEFUL EXPRESSIONS:

1. **Ohayō gozaimasu.** (Good morning.)
   おはようございます.
2. **Konnichi wa.** (Good afternoon.)
   こんにちは.
3. **Konban wa.** (Good evening.)
   こんばんは.
4. **Oyasumi nasai.** (Good night.)
   おやすみなさい.
5. **Sayōnara.** (Good-by.)
   さようなら.
6. **Sumimasen ga.**
   (Excuse me, but . . . (I have a request).)
   すみませんが.
7. **Dōmo arigatō gozaimasu.**
   (Thank you very much.)
   どうもありがとうございます.
8. **Dō itashimashite.**
   (You're welcome. Don't mention it.)
   どういたしまして.
9. **Wakarimasu ka?**
   (Do you understand?)
   分かりますか.
   Eigo ga wakarimasu ka?
   (Do you understand English?)
   英語が分かりますか.
10. **Hai** (Yes)
    はい.
    Hai, wakarimasu.
    (Yes, I understand.)
    はい, 分かります.
11. **Iie** (No)
    いいえ.
    Iie, wakarimasen.
    (No, I don't understand.)
    いいえ, 分かりません.
12. **Mō ichi-do itte kudasai.**
    (Please say (that) once more.)
    もう一度言ってください.

7

USEFUL EXPRESSIONS (cont.):

13. Motto yukkuri itte kudasai.
(Please speak more slowly.)
もっとゆっくり言ってください.

14. Hajimemashite.
(How do you do. Lit: It is the first time.)
はじめまして.

15. Onamae wa?
(What is your name?)
お名前は.

16. [Okusan] ni yoroshiku.
(My regards to [your wife].)
[奥さん] によろしく.

17. Mata aimashō.
(See you later.)
また会いましょう.

18. Gomen nasai.
(Excuse me.)
ごめんなさい.

19. Sumimasen.
(Excuse me. Pardon me.)
すみません.

20. Sō desu ka?
(Is that so?)
そうですか.

(O)tenki (weather (お) 天気)

Ame (Rain 雨)

Yuki (Snow 雪)

Hare (Clear 晴)

Kumori (Cloudy 曇)

DIALOGS:

Jones: Ogenki desu ka?
          (How are you? Lit: Are you healthy?)
          お元気ですか.
Tanaka: Hai, genki desu.   Okagesama de.
          (I'm fine, thank you.   Lit: Yes, I'm healthy,
          thanks to you.)
          はい, 元気です. おかげさまで.

Tanaka: Doko kara kimashita ka?
          (Where did you come from?)
          どこから来ましたか.
Jones: Amerika kara desu.
          (I came from America.)
          アメリカからです.
Tanaka: Itsu Nihon e kimashita ka?
          (When did you come to Japan?)
          いつ日本へ来ましたか.
Jones: [Ni]-shūkan mae desu.
          ([Two] weeks ago.)
          [二] 週間前です.
Tanaka: Nihongo ga ojōzu desu nē.
          (You speak Japanese very well.)
          日本語がお上手ですね.
Jones: Iie, mada heta desu.
          (No, I'm still poor (at speaking Japanese).)
          いいえ, まだへたです.

Jones: Kanai desu.
          (This is my wife.)
          家内です.
Mrs. Jones: Hajimete ome ni kakarimasu.   Dōzo yoro-
          shiku.
          (I am very happy to meet you.)
          はじめておめにかかります. どうぞよろしく.
Tanaka: Tanaka desu.   Dōzo yoroshiku.
          (I am Tanaka.   Glad to meet you.   Lit:
          Please (treat our relationship) well.)
          田中です. どうぞよろしく.

2 Taking a Taxi

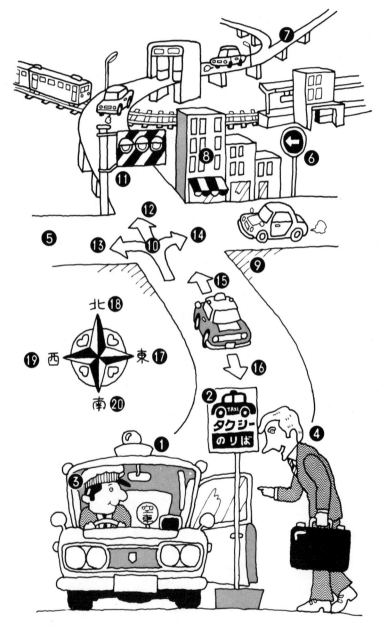

❶ **ta-ku-shi-i** (taxi)*
タクシー

❷ **ta-ku-shi-i no-ri-ba** (taxi stand)*
タクシーのりば／タクシー乗り場

❸ **u-n-te-n-shu(-sa-n)** (driver)
うんてんしゅ（さん）／運転手（さん）

❹ **jō-kya-ku** (passenger)
じょうきゃく／乗客

❺ **mi-chi** (road, street)
みち／道

❻ **i-ppō-tsū-kō** (one-way traffic)
いっぽうつうこう／一方通行

❼ **kō-so-ku-dō-ro** (expressway)
こうそくどうろ／高速道路

❽ **ta-te-mo-no** (building)
たてもの／建物

❾ **ka-do** (corner)
かど／角

❿ **kō-sa-te-n** (intersection)
こうさてん／交差点

⓫ **shi-n-gō** (traffic light)
しんごう／信号

⓬ **ma-ssu-gu** (straight)
まっすぐ

⓭ **hi-da-ri** (left)
ひだり／左

⓮ **mi-gi** (right)
みぎ／右

⓯ **u-shi-ro** (back)
うしろ／後

⓰ **ma-e** (front)
まえ／前

⓱ **hi-ga-shi** (east)
ひがし／東

⓲ **ki-ta** (north)
きた／北

⓳ **ni-shi** (west)
にし／西

⓴ **mi-na-mi** (south)
みなみ／南

11

NOTES:

*❶ **takushii:** Taxis can usually be flagged down anywhere by simply raising your hand, but in the late evening it sometimes becomes necessary to offer something extra in order to get a cab to pick you up, especially in entertainment districts.   Charging extra is, of course, an illegal practice, and is not to be encouraged.   Ask an **omawarisan** (policeman お巡りさん) for assistance if you have taxi troubles.

An empty taxi will display a red "flag" or light in the window to the left of the driver.   This "flag" (which lights up at night) contains the word **kūsha** (vacant car 空車).   The driver will pull the "flag" down to start the meter after you get in.   By the way, be careful of that door— the driver will open and close it for you automatically from his seat.   So stand aside.

*❷ **takushii noriba:** Taxi stands are located in front of most hotels, stations, and other places where crowds may congregate.

Takushii noriba (Taxi stand, see ❷)

ADDITIONAL WORDS:

tsukiatari (dead end 突きあたり)
kōban (police box 交番)
saki (ahead 先)
dōzo (please どうぞ)
kaisō (in transit 回送)

When a sign with the word *kaisō* is displayed in the window of a taxi, it will not pick up passengers.

Kōban (Police box)

USEFUL EXPRESSIONS:

1. **[Teikoku Hoteru] made onegai shimasu.**
   (Please (go) to [the Imperial Hotel].)
   [帝国ホテル] までお願いします.

2. **iku** (to go)
   行く.
   Massugu itte kudasai.
   (Please go straight.)
   まっすぐ行ってください.

3. **magaru** (to turn)
   曲がる.
   Tsugi no kado o migi e magatte kudasai.
   (Please turn right at the next corner.)
   次の角を右へ曲がってください.

4. **tomeru** (to stop)
   止める
   Koko (asoko) de tomete kudasai.
   (Please stop here (there).)
   ここ（あそこ）で止めてください.
   Eki no mae de tomete kudasai.
   (Please stop in front of the station.)
   駅の前で止めてください.

5. **yukkuri** (slowly)
   ゆっくり
   Motto yukkuri itte kudasai.
   (Please go more slowly.)
   もっとゆっくり行ってください.

6. **isogu** (to hurry)
   急ぐ
   Isoide kudasai.
   (Please hurry.)
   急いでください.

DIALOGS:

(At the station)

Jones: **Sumimasen ga, takushii noriba wa doko desu ka?**
(Excuse me, but where is the taxi stand?)
すみませんが，タクシー乗り場はどこですか.

Stranger: **Minami-guchi no mae da to omoimasu ga.**
(I think it's in front of the south exit, but ...
(I'm not sure).)
南口の前だと思いますが.

Jones: **Dōmo arigatō.**
(Thanks a lot.)
どうもありがとう.

(To the taxi driver)

Jones: **Kabukiza made itte kudasai.**
(Please go to the Kabukiza.)
歌舞伎座まで行ってください.

Driver: **Hai, wakarimashita.**
(Yes, sir. Lit: Yes, I understand.)
はい，分かりました.

(At the Kabukiza)

Driver: **Kabukiza desu.**
(This is the Kabukiza.)
歌舞伎座です.

Jones: **Ikura desu ka?**
(How much is it?)
いくらですか.

Driver: **Yonhyaku-gojū-en ni narimasu.**
(That will be 450 yen.)
四百五十円になります.

Jones: **Hai, gohyaku-en.**
(Here's 500 yen.)
はい，五百円.

Driver: **Otsuri desu.**
(Your change.)
おつりです.

3 Buying a Ticket at the Station

① **e-ki** (station)
えき／駅

② **ki-ppu** (ticket)*
きっぷ／切符

③ **ō-fu-ku ki-ppu** (round-trip ticket)
おうふくきっぷ／往復切符

④ **nyū-jō-ke-n** (platform ticket)*
にゅうじょうけん／入場券

⑤ **shi-te-i-ken** (reserved ticket)
していけん／指定券

⑥ **ka-i-sū-ken** (coupon ticket)*
かいすうけん／回数券

⑦ **te-i-ki-ke-n** (season ticket)*
ていきけん／定期券

❽ **ki-ppu u-ri-ba** (ticket-selling area)
きっぷうりば／切符売場

❾ **ke-n-ba-i-ki** (ticket-vending machine)*
けんばいき／券売機

❿ **mi-do-ri no ma-do-gu-chi** (Green Window)*
みどりのまどぐち／みどりの窓口

⑪ **za-se-ki ba-n-gō** (seat number)
ざせきばんごう／座席番号

⑫ **[sa-n]-gō-sha** (car number [three])
[さん]ごうしゃ／[三]号車

⑬ **i-ri-gu-chi** (entrance)
いりぐち／入口

⑭ **de-gu-chi** (exit)
でぐち／出口

⑮ **ka-i-sa-tsu-gu-chi** (wicket)
かいさつぐち／改札口   「cloakroom)*

⓰ **te-ni-mo-tsu i-chi-ji a-zu-ka-ri-jo** (checkroom,
てにもついちじあずかりじょ／手荷物一時預り所

⓱ **ko-i-n ro-kkā** (coin locker)
コインロッカー

⓲ **ni-mo-tsu** (luggage)
にもつ／荷物

⓳ **ba-su a-n-na-i-jo** (bus information booth)
バスあんないじょ／バス案内所

⓴ **ba-su no te-i-ryū-jo** (bus stop)
バスのていりゅうじょ／バスの停留所

NOTES:

*❷ **kippu**: Tickets for short distances are usually sold from vending machines, while those for longer distances must be purchased at the ticket window. Transfer tickets (good for one transfer from the national to a private railroad or vice versa) may also be purchased at the ticket window.

For children up to six years of age who are accompanied by their parents, tickets are not necessary. For children from six to twelve, the fare is half price, so be sure to get the special **kodomo no kippu** (children's tickets 子供の切符).

*❹ **nyūjōken**: Platform tickets allow you to go on the platform (to see a friend off, or to welcome an arriving friend), but do not allow you to ride on the train.

*❻ **kaisūken**: Coupon tickets are a kind of discount ticket. Eleven train coupon tickets may be bought for the price of ten regular tickets. All eleven tickets are connected together in a single sheet, and they should not be separated until after each ticket is punched when entering the platform area. They are good only between designated stations, and they must be used within a specified period of time. Bus coupon tickets are also available.

*❼ **teikiken**: For the commuter, the season ticket is the cheapest way to go. Within the specified period of time, the bearer may use his season ticket as frequently as he wishes between the stations designated on it. Depending on how often it is used, the commuter may save nearly half of the cost of regular tickets. Students make even greater savings since they may purchase season tickets at reduced rates.

*❾ **kenbaiki**: Ticket-vending machines are easy to use once you determine the price of the ticket you want (ask someone if you cannot figure out the map at the station). Simply drop sufficient coins to cover the cost of the ticket into a machine marked for that amount. If the machine dispenses tickets of various amounts, you must also press the button for the price of the ticket you want.

Change, if any, will come out with the ticket.

*⓾ **midori no madoguchi:** Green Window is the term used by the Japanese National Railways to indicate the place where reserved seat tickets, *shinkansen* and other long distance train tickets, etc. may be purchased.

*⓰ **tenimotsu ichiji azukarijo:** Another common name for the checkroom is **keitaihin azukarijo** (checkroom, cloakroom 携帯品預り所). Whichever name is used, these places allow you to check your luggage for a day or so.

ADDITIONAL WORDS:

kankō basu (tour bus 観光バス)
[go]-ban no basu (bus number [five] [5] 番のバス)
toden (metropolitan streetcar 都電)
shiden (city streetcar 市電)

Kaisūken (Coupon tickets, see ❻)

Teikiken (Season ticket, see ❼)

USEFUL EXPRESSIONS:

1. **[Kyōto] made no kippu o san-mai kudasai.**
   (Please give me three tickets for [Kyoto].)
   [京都] までの切符を 3 枚ください.

2. **[Shinjuku] made ikura desu ka?**
   (How much is it to [Shinjuku]?)
   [新宿] までいくらですか.

3. **[Shibuya] made no kaisūken o kudasai.**
   (Please give me some coupon tickets for [Shibuya].)
   [渋谷] までの回数券をください.

4. **basu** (bus)
   バス
   Basu no annaijo wa doko desu ka?
   (Where is the bus information booth?)
   バスの案内所はどこですか.

5. **keiyu** (via)
   経由
   Kono basu wa [Roppongi] keiyu no [Tōkyō Eki]-yuki desu ka?
   (Does this bus go to [Tokyo Station] via [Roppongi]?)
   このバスは [六本木] 経由の [東京駅] 行きですか.

6. **tōru** (to go through)
   通る
   Kono basu wa [Ginza yon-chōme] o tōrimasu ka?
   (Does this bus go through [Ginza 4-chōme]?)
   このバスは [銀座四丁目] を通りますか.

Kaisatsuguchi (Wicket, see ⓯)

Midori no madoguchi
(Green Window, see  ⑩) sign

DIALOG:

(At the Green Window)

Jones: **Hikari wa Atami ni tomarimasu ka?**
(Does the Hikari stop at Atami?)
ひかりは熱海に止まりますか.

Clerk: **Iie, tomarimasen ga, Kodama wa tomarimasu**
(No, it doesn't, but the Kodama does.)
いいえ, 止まりませんがこだまは止まります.

Jones: **Tsugi no Kodama no shiteiken arimasu ka?**
(Do you have any reserved tickets for the next Kodama?)
つぎのこだまの指定券ありますか.

Clerk: **Iie, mō urikiremashita ga, jiyūseki nara arimasu.**
(No, they're sold out, but we have some unreserved seat (tickets).)
いいえ, もう売り切れましたが自由席ならあります.

Jones: **Dewa Atami made, jiyūseki no kippu o ni-mai kudasai.**
(Well, give me two unreserved seat tickets for Atami.)
では熱海まで自由席の切符を2枚ください.

COUNTER:

-mai (thin, flat objects 一枚)
This counter is used for things like tickets, *furoshiki*, sheets, blankets, plates, paper, etc.

ichi-mai	一枚	one thin, flat object
ni-mai	二枚	two thin, flat objects
san-mai	三枚	three thin, flat objects
yon-mai	四枚	four thin, flat objects.

4 Taking a Train

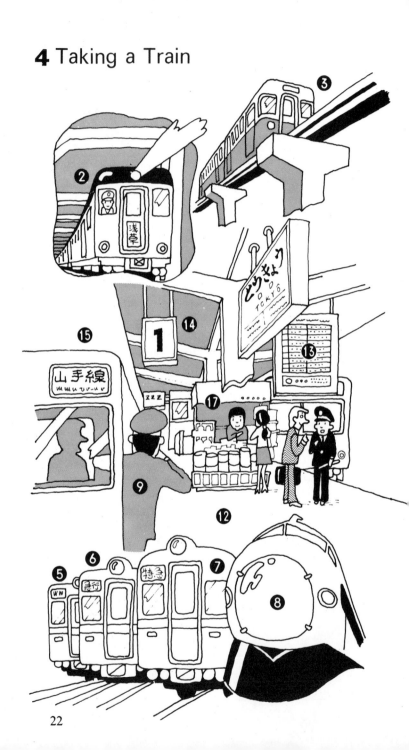

① **de-n-sha** (train)
でんしゃ／電車

❷ **chi-ka-te-tsu** (subway)
ちかてつ／地下鉄

❸ **mo-no-rē-ru** (monorail)
モノレール

④ **ka-ku-e-ki te-i-sha** (local train)
かくえきていしゃ／各駅停車

❺ **ju-n-kyū** (limited express)*
じゅんきゅう／準急

❻ **kyū-kō** (express)*
きゅうこう／急行

❼ **to-kkyū** (special express)*
とっきゅう／特急

❽ **shi-n-ka-n-se-n** (Bullet Train)*
しんかんせん／新幹線

❾ **sha-shō** (conductor)
しゃしょう／車掌

⑩ **ko-ku-te-tsu** (national railroad, JNR)*
こくてつ／国鉄

⑪ **shi-te-tsu** (private railroad)*
してつ／私鉄

❿ **hō-mu** (platform)
ホーム

⓭ **re-ssha ji-ko-ku-hyō** (train schedule)
れっしゃじこくひょう／列車時刻表

⓮ **[i-chi]-ba-n-se-n** (track number [one])
[いち] ばんせん／[1] 番線

⓯ **[Ya-ma-no-te]-se-n** ([Yamanote] line)*
[やまのて] せん／[山の手] 線

⑯ **e-ki-chō-shi-tsu** (station master's office) *
えきちょうしつ／駅長室

⓱ **e-ki no bai-te-n** (station shop, newsstand)*
えきのばいてん／駅の売店

⑱ **e-ki-be-n** (station lunch)*
えきべん／駅弁

⑲ **shu-ppa-tsu** (departure)
しゅっぱつ／出発

⑳ **tō-cha-ku** (arrival)
とうちゃく／到着

NOTES:

*❺ **junkyū:** A limited express train stops at fewer stations than a local train, but at more than an express.

*❻ **kyūkō:** Faster than the limited express, the express train will stop at only the more important stations.

*❼ **tokkyū:** *Tokkyū* is the short way of saying **tokubetsu kyūkō** (special express 特別急行). The special express will stop at only the most important of stations, and it often requires a special ticket called a **tokkyūken** (special express ticket 特急券) in addition to the usual ticket.

*❽ **shinkansen:** Recently the Japanese National Railways has let it be known that they want the Bullet Train to be known by its Japanese name, the *shinkansen*. But whichever name you use, it is still the world's fastest passenger train in service. There are two types, the *Hikari* and the *Kodama*. The Hikari stops at the fewest stations, while the Kodama makes more frequent stops. Currently the line extends from Tokyo to Kyoto, Osaka, and beyond to Hakata, but plans have been made to lay *shinkansen* tracks throughout Japan.

*❿ **kokutetsu:** The national railroad, officially known as the Japanese National Railways (JNR), operates most long distance trains in Japan, including the *shinkansen*.

*⓫ **shitetsu:** Private railroads extend into nearly every corner of Japan, wherever the national railroad doesn't go.

*⓯ **Yamanote-sen:** The different lines in Tokyo employ different color schemes for easy recognition: the *Yamanote* line uses green, the *Chūō* line is orange, the *Keihintōhoku* line uses blue, the *Sōbu* line is yellow, etc.

*⓰ **ekichōshitsu:** In the station master's office you will find the **ekichō** (station master 駅長). The person who signals the conductor and pushes passengers on the crowded rush-hour trains is called **ekiin** (station employee 駅員).

*⓱ **eki no baiten:** Recently the Japanese National Railways has begun to call the station shop a *kiosk*.

Regardless of the name, these shops sell a variety of items, including newspapers and magazines, tissue paper, milk, beer, candy, cigarettes and ball point pens.

*⑱ **ekiben:** A station lunch is simply an **(o)bentō** (Japanese-style box lunch (お)弁当) which is sold at the station. It is a great favorite with Japanese travelers for whom eating is the most common way to pass the time on long train rides. At certain stations, especially tasty *ekiben* (made from the special products of the region nearby) can be purchased.

ADDITIONAL WORDS:

shindaisha (sleeping car 寝台車)
guriinsha (Green Car グリーン車)
    This is a special car on some long distance trains for first-class reserved seats only.
akabō (redcap, porter 赤帽)

Eki no baiten
(Station shop, see ⑰)

Ekiin (Station employee, see note⑯) packing a rush-hour train

USEFUL EXPRESSIONS:

1. **tsugi**   (next)
   つぎ
   Tsugi wa [Tōkyō] desu.
   (The next (station) is [Tokyo].)
   つぎは [東京] です.

2. **noru**   (to get on)
   乗る
   Kono densha wa konde iru kara, tsugi no ni norimashō.
   (Since this train is crowded, let's get on the next one.)
   この電車は混んでいるから次のに乗りましょう.

3. **oriru**   (to get off)
   降りる
   Orimasu!   (I'm getting off!)
   降ります.

4. **norikaeru**   (to transfer)
   乗り換える
   Doko de norikaeru no desu ka?
   (Where do I have to transfer?)
   どこで乗り換えるのですか.

5. **shūten**   (terminal station, end of the line)
   終点
   Tsugi wa [Tōkyō Eki], shūten desu.
   (Next is [Tokyo Station], the end of the line.)
   次は [東京駅] 終点です.

6. **Kono chikatetsu wa [Ginza] e ikimasu ka?**
   (Does this subway go to the [Ginza]?)
   この地下鉄は [銀座] へ行きますか.

7. **tomaru**   (to stop (at))
   止まる
   Kono densha wa [Yoyogi] ni tomarimasu ka?
   (Does this train stop at [Yoyogi] (Station)?)
   この電車は [代々木] に止まりますか.

8. **haraimodoshi**   (refund)
   払い戻し
   Haraimodoshi shite kudasai.
   (Please refund (the price of this ticket).)
   払い戻ししてください.

DIALOG:

Jones: **Kono tsugi no Hikari wa nanbansen desu ka?**
(What track is the next Hikari (leaving from)?)
このつぎのひかりは何番線ですか.

Station
Employee: **[Jūgo]-bansen desu.**
(Track number [15].)
[15]番線です

(On the platform of track 15)

Jones: **[San]-gōsha wa doko desu ka?**
(Where is car number [3]?)
[3]号車はどこですか.

Employee: **Mae no hō desu.**
(It's toward the front (of the train).)
前の方です.

Jones: **Shokudōsha ga arimasu ka?**
(Is there a dining car?)
食堂車がありますか.

Employee: **Hai, arimasu. [Go]-gōsha desu.**
(Yes, there is. It's car number [5].)
はいあります. [5]号車です.

Shinkansen (Bullet Train, see ❽)   Picture courtesy of JNTO

5 Checking In and Out

❶ **ho-te-ru** (hotel)
ホテル

❷ **ryo-ka-n** (Japanese inn)*
りょかん／旅館

③ **mi-n-shu-ku** (family inn)*
みんしゅく／民宿

④ **yū-su-ho-su-te-ru** (youth hostel)*
ユースホステル

⑤ **yo-ya-ku** (reservation)
よやく／予約

⑥ **ma-e-ki-n** (deposit)
まえきん／前金

❼ **he-ya** (room)
へや／部屋

⑧ **da-bu-ru rū-mu** (double room)
ダブルルーム

❾ **shi-n-gu-ru rū-mu** (single room)
シングルルーム

❿ **(o-)fu-ro** (bath)
（お)ふろ／（お)風呂

⓫ **(o-)te-a-ra-i, to-i-re** (washroom, toilet)*
（お)てあらい／お手洗い，トイレ

⑫ **re-i-bō** (air conditioning)
れいぼう／冷房

⑬ **da-n-bō** (heating)
だんぼう／暖房

⓮ **fu-ro-n-to** (front desk)
フロント

⓯ **ro-bi-i** (lobby)
ロビー

⓰ **ma-ne-jā, shi-ha-i-ni-n** (manager)
マネジャー，しはいにん／支配人

⑰ **che-kku-a-u-to no ji-ka-n** (check-out time)
チェックアウトのじかん／チェックアウトの時間

⑱ **ka-n-jō** (bill)
かんじょう／勘定

⑲ **u-ke-to-ri** (receipt)
うけとり／受取

⑳ **[i-k]ka-i** ([first] floor)
[いっ]かい／[一]階

NOTES:

*❷ **ryokan:** The Japanese inn will give the traveler a taste of Japanese living which hotels cannot provide. Guests live on traditional *tatami* mats during their stay, eat typical Japanese meals, take a leisurely Japanese bath, and sleep in the comfortable Japanese *futon*.

*❸ **minshuku:** *Minshuku* literally means "people's inn" and refers to privately owned establishments which receive overnight guests. *Minshuku* are commonly run as a side business by the families of farmers or fishermen who wish to supplement their incomes. When compared to hotels and Japanese inns, *minshuku* rates are very reasonable, and they include both dinner and breakfast. Rooms are notably simple, and guests must spread a *futon* for themselves before going to bed at night and pick it up again in the morning. However, the meals include the freshest of vegetables and fish, are truly home-cooked, and are the finest available in Japan.

If you wish to stay at a *minshuku*, you must make reservations (preferably at least a month in advance) with **Nihon Minshuku Kyōkai** (Japan *Minshuku* Association 日本民宿協会). Reservations must be made in person so that a deposit may be paid. The main office in Tokyo is located in the basement of the Kōtsūkaikan building near Yūrakuchō Station:

Kōtsūkaikan	東京都千代田区
2-13, Yūrakuchō	有楽町2-13
Chiyoda-ku, Tokyo	交通会館内
(Tel: 216-6556)	

Other offices are located in the underground shopping area outside of the Yaesu Entrance to Tokyo Station, on the first floor of the Parco store in Ikebukuro, and on the fifth floor of the Parco store in Shibuya. In Osaka, reservations may be made at the office in the Dōjima underground shopping area, telephone 345-2101. Needless to say, Japanese is more than helpful.

*❹ **yūsuhosuteru:** There are over 500 youth hostels located in every part of Japan, and they are undoubtedly the cheapest accommodations available. Overnight rates including two meals are very inexpensive. Tourists in Japan may not become members of the Youth Hostel Association, so it is best to make those arrangements in your home country. (However, a few youth hostels are open to non-members also.) If you live in Japan, membership fee for individuals vary according to age, but are always very reasonable. Family memberships are also available.

For further information about hostel locations and reservation procedures, contact the Tokyo Youth Hostels Association near the Toranomon Station on the Ginza Line subway:

> Nihon Shōbō Kaikan, 4F
> 18, Nishikubo Akefune-chō, Shiba
> Minato-ku, Tokyo
> (Tel: 501-5873)
> 東京都ユースホステル協会
> 東京都港区芝西久保明舟町18
> 日本消防会館4階

Other offices are located on the sixth floor of Sogō Department Store in Yūrakuchō and on the sixth floor of Keiō Department Store in Shinjuku. In Osaka, the place to contact is the Osaka Youth Hostels Association:

> 1436, Kuramae-chō   大阪ユースホステル協会
> Naniwa-ku, Osaka-shi   大阪市浪速区蔵前1436
> (Tel: 633-8621)

*⓫ (o)tearai, toire: While Western-style restroom facilities are available in hotels, large restaurants and other places that cater to foreign tourists, there are occasions when you may have to use a Japanese toilet (for instance, in *minshuku*). It is usual to squat over, not sit on, the Japanese toilet, facing in the direction of the "cup" which rises above the floor. Since no part of the body comes in contact with the toilet, many people consider it more sanitary than the Western-style toilet. If you use a public toilet, it may be necessary to supply your own **chirigami** (tissue paper ちり紙), since toilet paper is not always provided.

Many small restaurants, bars, and other establishments have only one small toilet for use by both men and

Japanese-style **toire**
(Toilet, see **11**)

Put your feet in the
slippers and squat.

Yūsuhosuteru (Youth hostel, see **4**)

women.   Knock on the door before entering; if someone
is inside, he will knock back at you.   In cases where there
is a urinal as well as a toilet, it is not uncommon for a
woman to enter and nonchalantly walk past a man using
the urinal in order to reach the toilet compartment.
Don't be surprised; after all, it's only nature calling.

USEFUL EXPRESSIONS:

1. **Konban aite iru heya wa arimasu ka?**
   (Do you have any vacant rooms this evening?)
   　　今晩空いている部屋はありますか.
2. **Furo-tsuki no heya wa arimasu ka?**
   (Do you have a room with a bath?)
   　　風呂つきの部屋はありますか.
3. **Chekku-auto no jikan wa nanji desu ka?**
   (What is the check-out time?)
   　　チェックアウトの時間は何時ですか.
4. **Ashita no asa shichi-ji ni okoshite kudasai.**
   (Please wake me at 7 o'clock tomorrow morning.)
   　　あしたの朝七時に起こしてください.
5. **Maekin wa irimasu ka?**
   (Do you require a deposit?)
   　　前金はいりますか.

DIALOGS:

(Checking in)

Jones: **Konban yoyaku shita Jōnzu desu.**

(My name is Jones and I have a reservation for tonight.)

今晩予約したジョーンズです.

Clerk: **Jōnzu-san desu ka? Jukkai no shinguru rūmu de yoroshii desu ka?**

(Mr. Jones. Is a single room on the tenth floor all right?)

ジョーンズさんですか. 十階のシングルルームでよろしいですか.

Jones: **Motto ue no kai no heya ni shite moraitai n desu ga.**

(Could you give me a room on a higher floor, if …(it is possible)?)

もっと上の階の部屋にしてもらいたいんですが.

Clerk: **Nijūgo-kai wa ikaga desu ka?**

(How about on the 25th floor?)

25階はいかがですか.

Jones: **Kekkō desu.**

(That'll be fine.)

けっこうです.

(Checking out)

Jones: **Kanjō o onegai shimasu.**

(Please give me my bill.)

勘定をお願いします.

Clerk: **Hai. Yoku nemuremashita ka?**

(Here you are. Did you have a good night's sleep?)

はい. よく眠れましたか.

Jones: **Hai, yoku nemuremashita.**

(Yes, I slept very well.)

はい, よく眠れました.

Clerk: **Dōmo arigatō gozaimashita. Mata dō**

(Thank you very much. Please com)

どうもありがとうございました. ま

33

❶ **ta-ta-mi** (*tatami* mat)*
 たたみ／畳

❷ **fu-to-n** (Japanese bed)*
 ふとん／蒲団

❸ **shi-ki-bu-to-n** (mattress)*
 しきぶとん／敷蒲団

❹ **shi-ki-fu** (sheet)*
 しきふ／敷布

❺ **ka-ke-bu-to-n** (quilt, bedcover)*
 かけぶとん／掛蒲団

⑥ **mō-fu** (blanket)*
 もうふ／毛布

❼ **ma-ku-ra** (pillow)*
 まくら／枕

❽ **za-bu-to-n** (floor cushion)*
 ざぶとん／座蒲団

⑨ **chō-sho-ku** (breakfast)
 ちょうしょく／朝食

⑩ **yū-sho-ku** (dinner)
 ゆうしょく／夕食

⓫ **o-cha** (tea)
 おちゃ／お茶

⓬ **ma-do** (window)
 まど／窓

⓭ **ta-o-ru** (towel)
 タオル

⓮ **ha-n-gā** (hanger)
 ハンガー

⓯ **yu-ka-ta** (light cotton *kimono*)*
 ゆかた／浴衣

⑯ **ka-gi** (key)
 かぎ／鍵

⑰ **rū-mu sā-bi-su** (room service)
 ルーム・サービス

⑱ **he-ya no ba-n-gō** (room number)
 へやのばんごう／部屋の番号

⑲ **(o-)kya-ku(-sa-n)** (guest)
 （お）きゃく（さん）／（お）客（さん）

⓴ **jo-chū(-sa-n)** (maid)
 じょちゅう（さん）／女中（さん）

NOTES:

*❶ **tatami:** The floor of a traditional Japanese room is covered by a reed mat called *tatami*. Be sure to remove your slippers before stepping on *tatami* mats. (See also the note on page 156.)

*❷ **futon:** The Japanese bed is placed on *tatami* mats at night when you retire, and it is taken up again in the morning after you get up.

*❸ **shikibuton:** To spread a *futon*, one or two mattresses are first placed on the *tatami* mats. When two mattresses are used, the first is usually filled with foam rubber, while the one on top of it is the more traditional cotton-stuffed mattress.

*❹ **shikifu:** Next a sheet is put over the *shikibuton*.

*❺ **kakebuton:** Finally comes the bedcover, or quilt, which is itself covered by a special sheet. In cold weather, two or more *kakebuton* are used.

*❻ **mōfu:** Blankets may also be added if desired (before the *kakebuton*), especially in cold weather. In warm weather, the blanket may be used alone (no *kakebuton*).

*❼ **makura:** The Japanese pillow is small and rather hard as it is filled with **sobagara** (buckwheat chaff そば殻) or a modern substitute.

*❽ **zabuton:** These floor cushions are used instead of chairs in *tatami* rooms.

*⓯ **yukata:** Worn in summer, the cotton *kimono* is very comfortable after a hot bath. Most *ryokan* provide fresh *yukata* for their guests. (See also the note on page 146.)

USEFUL EXPRESSIONS:

1. **Samui n desu ga, kakebuton o mō ichi-mai kashite kudasai.**

   (It's cold, so could you give me another quilt.)

   寒いんですが掛蒲団をもう一枚貸してください.

Futon (Japanese bed, see ❷) Picture courtesy of JNTO

2. **Ofuro wa mō waite imasu ka.**
   (Is the bath hot yet?)
   　お風呂はもう沸いていますか.

3. **Toire wa doko ni arimasu ka?**
   (Where is the toilet?)
   　トイレはどこにありますか.

4. **Mō ichi-nichi tomaremasu ka?**
   (Can I stay one more day?)
   　もう一日泊まれますか.

DIALOG:

(At a *minshuku*)

Farmer: **Konnichi wa.　Yoku irasshaimashita.**
(Good afternoon.　Welcome (to this *minshuku*).)
　こんにちは. よくいらっしゃいました.

Jones: **Konnichi wa.　Jōnzu desu.　Osewa ni narimasu.**
(Good afternoon.　I am Jones.　Thank you for your assistance.)
　こんにちは. ジョーンズです. お世話になります.

Farmer: **Kochira e dōzo.　Otsukare deshō.　Sugu ofuro ni ohairi ni narimasu ka?**
(This way, please.　You are probably tired. Will you take a bath soon?)
　こちらへどうぞ. お疲れでしょう. すぐお風呂にお入りになりますか.

Jones: **Hai, onegai shimasu.**
(Yes, please.)
　はい, お願いします.

7 At the Restaurant

❶ re-su-to-ra-n (restaurant)
レストラン

② **ni-ho-n ryō-ri-ya** (Japanese restaurant)*
にほんりょうりや／日本料理屋

③ **chū-ka ryō-ri-te-n** (Chinese restaurant)*
ちゅうかりょうりてん／中華料理店

④ **bi-ya hō-ru** (beer hall)
ビヤホール

⑤ **sho-ku-dō** (dining room, mess hall)
しょくどう／食堂

⑥ **se-i-yō ryō-ri** (Western cooking)
せいようりょうり／西洋料理

❼ u-e-i-tā (waiter)
ウェイター

❽ u-e-i-to-re-su (waitress)
ウェイトレス

⑨ **te-i-sho-ku** (table d'hôte)*
ていしょく／定食

⑩ **sho-kke-n** (meal ticket)*
しょくけん／食券

⓫ tē-bu-ru (table)
テーブル

⓬ **i-su** (chair)
いす／椅子

⓭ **o-shi-bo-ri** (wet towel for cleaning hands)*
おしぼり

⓮ **hō-ku** (fork)
フォーク

⓯ **su-pū-n** (spoon)
スプーン

⓰ **na-i-fu** (knife)
ナイフ

⓱ **ko-ppu** (glass)
コップ

⓲ **(o-)sa-ra** (plate)
（お）さら／（お）皿

⑲ **na-pu-ki-n** (napkin)
ナプキン

⑳ **yō-ji** (toothpick)
ようじ／楊枝

NOTES:

*❷ **nihon ryōriya**: The word *ryōri* means "cooking." The suffix *-ya* means "shop" or "store" and is often placed after the name of a food to indicate the place where it may be bought or eaten.

*❸ **chūka ryōriten**: *Chūka ryōri* means "Chinese cooking" and the suffix *-ten* is used instead of *-ya* but means the same thing, a "store" or a "shop."

*❾ **teishoku**: A typical table d'hôte, or complete meal, at a Japanese restaurant might include **miso shiru** (bean paste soup 味噌汁), **gohan** (rice ご飯), and *tsukemono*, along with the main item of the order. One of the great advantages of the *teishoku* is that it is usually cheaper.

*❿ **shokken**: Meal tickets are used in certain types of restaurants, especially *shokudō* and *rāmen* shops. The tickets should be purchased at the entrance before you sit down.

*⓭ **oshibori**: Most tourists in Japan find the *oshibori* a delightful custom. It is a small towel served either steaming hot or refreshingly cold when the customer sits down at his table. It is used to wipe the sweat from the face and the dirt from the hands before eating.

Shokudō (Dining room, see ❺)
entrance

ADDITIONAL WORDS:

(o)satō (sugar 砂糖)
(o)shio (salt（お）塩)
koshō (pepper コショウ)
kōhii (coffee コーヒー)
kōcha (black tea 紅茶)
ocha (green tea お茶)
amai (sweet 甘い)
nigai (bitter 苦い)
suppai (sour 酸っぱい)
koi (strong, thick 濃い)
usui (weak, thin うすい)
atsui (hot 熱い)
tsumetai (cold 冷たい)

USEFUL EXPRESSIONS:

1. **menyū** (menu)
   メニュー
   Menyū o misete kudasai.
   (Please show me a menu.)
   メニューを見せてください.

2. **Shinjuku no resutoran de tabemashō ka?**
   (Shall we eat at a restaurant in Shinjuku?)
   新宿のレストランで食べましょうか.

3. **(o)mizu** (water)
   (お)水
   Mizu o kudasai.
   (Please give me some water.)
   水をください.

4. **nodo ga kawaku** (to be thirsty)
   のどが渇く
   Nodo ga kawaita kara, nani ka nomimashō.
   (I am thirsty. Let's get something to drink.)
   のどが渇いたからなにか飲みましょう.

5. **onaka ga suku** (to be hungry)
   おなかがすく
   Onaka ga sukimashita ka?
   (Are you hungry?)
   おなかがすきましたか.

Oshibori (see ⓭)

DIALOG:

Tanaka: (To Jones) **Nani ni shimasu ka?**
(What would you like?)
何にしますか.

Jones: **Bifuteki ga oishisō desu ne.**
(Beefsteak looks good.)
ビフテキがおいしそうですね.

Tanaka: **Jā, sore ni shimashō.** (To waitress) **Bifuteki ni-ninmae onengai shimasu.**
(Yes, that looks good. (To waitress) Beefsteak for two, please.)
じゃあ，それにしましょう. ビフテキ二人前お願いします.

8 Eating and Drinking Japanese Style

42

① **te-n-pu-ra** (*tempura*, fried fish and vegetables)
てんぷら／天麩羅 「style)

❷ **su-ki-ya-ki** (*sukiyaki*, beef cooked Japanese
すきやき／すき焼き

❸ **su-shi** (*sushi*, vinegared rice with raw fish, etc.)*
すし／鮨

④ **u-do-n** (noodles)*
うどん

⑤ **so-ba** (buckwheat noodles)*
そば

❻ **sa-shi-mi** (raw fish)
さしみ／刺身

⑦ **u-na-gi** (eel)
うなぎ／鰻

⑧ **rā-me-n** (Chinese noodles)*
ラーメン

❾ **ya-ki-to-ri** (grilled chicken on a stick)*
やきとり／焼鳥

❿ **sa-ke** (*sake*, Japanese rice wine)*
さけ／酒

⓫ **tsu-ke-mo-no** (pickles)*
つけもの／漬物

⓬ **shō-yu** (soy sauce)
しょうゆ／醤油

⓭ **ka-ra-shi** (mustard)*
からし／芥子

⑭ **wa-sa-bi** (a kind of horseradish)
わさび／山葵

⓯ **cha-wa-n** (rice bowl)*
ちゃわん／茶碗

⓰ **ha-shi** (chopsticks)
はし／箸

⓱ **yu-no-mi-ja-wa-n** (teacup)
ゆのみじゃわん／湯呑茶碗

⓲ **cha-bi-n, do-bi-n** (teapot)
ちゃびん／茶瓶，どびん／土瓶

⓳ **(o-)cho-ko** (*sake* cup)*
（お）ちょこ／（お）猪口

⓴ **to-kku-ri** (*sake* pitcher)
とっくり／徳利

NOTES:

*❸ sushi: *Sushi* is served in many ways, but the most common is raw fish on top of vinegared rice with a dab of *wasabi* on it. *Sushi* is also served with various vegetables, seaweed, and egg "omelets" (instead of raw fish) over and around the vinegared rice. No one should leave Japan without having tried *sushi*, a most delicious treat and a peculiarly Japanese food. For a more complete description of *sushi* and other Japanese foods, read *Eating Cheap in Japan* by Kimiko Nagasawa and Camy Condon, published by Shufunotomo, 1972. Women use the polite *osushi*.

*❹ udon: The noodle for udon is made from wheat. Women use the polite *oudon*.

*❺ soba: *Soba* is the choice of people with health food preferences since the noodle is made from buckwheat. Women use the polite *osoba*.

*❽ rāmen: Besides the cheap Chinese noodles which may be eaten in a Chinese restaurant, there is another variety called **insutanto rāmen** (instant *rāmen* インスタント ラーメン) which may be purchased at any food market and taken home for quick preparation.

*❾ yakitori: *Yaki* literally means "burned" or "grilled," and *tori* means "fowl." Actually, however, other ingredients besides fowl (usually chicken) are used. When ordering, you should ask for **hinaniku** (young chicken meat ひな肉), **motsu** (liver もつ), **negi** (leek ねぎ), or **kawa** (skin (of the chicken) 皮). Whatever the ingredients of *yakitori*, they are cut in bits, skewered on a small bamboo stick, barbequed, and dipped in a special sauce. *Yakitori* can be purchased at a **yakitori-ya** (*yakitori* shop 焼き鳥屋) or at some **yatai** (street stand 屋台).

*❿ sake: *Sake* is a general term used for any alchoholic beverage, but it is particularly used for the traditional "rice wine" of Japan. Drinking *sake* properly approaches an art. *Sake* is normally heated before it is served and it is drunk while still warm. If it is somehow inconvenient to heat the *sake*, Japanese will also drink cold *sake*. You should never fill your own cup.

44

Rather, everyone fills everyone else's *choko*, never allowing another's cup to become empty. This is a simple and pleasant gesture of friendship which applies to beer and other social drinks as well. When having your own cup filled, be sure to hold it up to the pitcher as a gesture of acceptance. Before any one starts drinking, everyone will say **kanpai!** (a toast! 乾杯).

When purchasing *sake*, you may want to specify **tokkyū** (special class 特級), the top grade of *sake*; **ikkyū** (first class 一級), the second grade; or **ni-kyū** (second class 二級), the third grade. While usually sold in large **isshōbin** (a bottle of 1.8 liters 一升瓶) for home consumption, *sake* is also available in small bottles. Women use the polite term *osake*.

*⓫ **tsukemono**: This is a general term for pickled vegetables. The variety is wide, as is their appeal to the Japanese appetite, and they are served commonly with rice.

*⓭ **karashi**: This variety of mustard is extremely **karai** (hot, spicy 辛い) and it is recommended that you use it sparingly until you are familiar with its powers.

*⓯ **chawan**: This term may be used to mean a tea bowl also, depending on the situation (see Tea Ceremony and Flower Arrangement, p. 95).

*⓳ **(o)choko**: Besides the cup, Japanese will sometimes use a **masu** (small wooden measuring box ます) for drinking *sake*. Salt is placed on the edge of the box, and *sake* is drunk over it.

Left to right: isshōbin (see ❿)
tokkuri (see ⓴) choko and masu (see ⓳)

USEFUL EXPRESSIONS:

1. **mō ippai** (one more glass)
   もう一杯
   Sake o mō ippai kudasai.
   (Please give me one more cup of *sake*.)
   酒をもう一杯ください.
2. **mō ippon** (one more bottle (or long, thin object))
   もう一本
   Sake o mō ippon kudasai.
   (Please give me another pitcher of *sake*.)
   酒をもう一本ください.
   Biiru o mō ippon kudasai.
   (Please give me another bottle of beer.)
   ビールをもう一本ください.
   Yakitori o juppon kudasai.
   (Give me ten sticks of *yakitori*, please.)
   焼き鳥を十本ください.
3. **[ichi]-ninmae** ([one] serving)
   [一] 人前
   Tenpura o ichi-ninmae onegai shimasu.
   (Give me one serving of *tempura*, please.)
   天ぷらを一人前お願いします.

COUNTER:

-hon (long, cylindrical objects 一本)
   This counter is used for things like pens,
cigarettes, bottles, trees, etc.

ippon	一本	one long, cylindrical object
ni-hon	二本	two long, cylindrical objects
san-bon	三本	three long, cylindrical objects
yon-hon	四本	four long, cylindrical objects
go-hon	五本	five long, cylindrical objects
roppon	六本	six long, cylindrical objects

DIALOG:

Tanaka:	**Jōnzu-san, sake osuki desu ka?**
	(Mr. Jones, do you like *sake*?)
	ジョーンズさん，酒お好きですか.
Jones:	**Hai, daisuki desu.**
	(Yes, I like it very much.)
	はい，大好きです.
Tanaka:	**Konban ippai nomimasen ka.**
	(Shall we have a cup (of *sake*) tonight?)
	今晩いっぱい飲みませんか.
Jones:	**Ii desu nē.**
	(That sounds great.)
	いいですねえ.
Tanaka:	**Sushi-ya e ikimashō ka?**
	(Shall we go to a *sushi* shop?)
	すし屋へ行きましょうか.
Jones:	**Sushi mo ii desu ga, yakitori ga tabetai desu nē.**
	(*Sushi* is good too, but I'd like to have some *yakitori*.)
	すしもいいですが，焼き鳥が食べたいですねえ.
Tanaka:	**Sō desu ka. Ja, sō shimashō.**
	(Is that so? Well, let's do that.)
	そうですか. じゃあ，そうしましょう.

Yatai (Street stand, see note ❾)

9 At the Post Office

❶ yū-bi-n-kyo-ku (post office)
ゆうびんきょく／郵便局

❷ po-su-to (mail box, mail drop)*
ポスト

❸ te-ga-mi (letter)
てがみ／手紙

❹ fū-sho (sealed letter)
ふうしょ／封書

❺ ha-ga-ki (post card)
はがき／葉書

❻ e-ha-ga-ki (picture postcard)
えはがき／絵葉書

❼ ō-fu-ku ha-ga-ki (return postcard)
おうふくはがき／往復葉書

❽ fū-tō (envelope)
ふうとう／封筒

❾ kō-kū sho-ka-n (aerogram, air letter)
こうくうしょかん／航空書簡

⑩ jū-sho (address)
じゅうしょ／住所

❶ a-te-na (addressee's address)
あてな／宛名

⑫ ki-tte (stamp)*
きって／切手

⓭ ko-zu-tsu-mi (parcel, package)*
こづつみ／小包

⓮ ko-ga-ta hō-sō-bu-tsu (small packet)*
こがたほうそうぶつ／小形包装物

⑮ kō-kū-bi-n (airmail)
こうくうびん／航空便

⑯ fu-na-bi-n (seamail)
ふなびん／船便

⑰ so-ku-ta-tsu (special delivery)
そくたつ／速達

⑱ ka-ki-to-me (registered mail)
かきとめ／書留

⑲ i-n-sa-tsu-bu-tsu (printed matter)
いんさつぶつ／印刷物

⓴ ko-wa-re-mo-no (fragile article)
こわれもの／こわれ物

NOTES:

*❷ **posuto:** In metropolitan areas of Japan, the mail box is usually red-orange and has two mail slots. The slot on the right is for regular, local mail, while the one on the left is for all other mail (out-of-town mail, airmail, special delivery, etc.). Sometimes a blue mail box is used for the same mail as is usually put in the left slot of a regular mail box. In rural areas, there is usually a single-slot mail box (looking something like a large, red-orange fire hydrant) for all mail.

*⓬ **kitte:** Philatelists will want to ask for **kinen kitte** (commemorative stamps 記念切手).

*⓭ **kozutsumi:** Only the larger post offices handle packages; smaller ones are not equipped to do so. You will need to fill out a **zeikan kokuchisho** (customs declaration 税関告知書) for such packages. The weight limit is usually ten kilograms.

*⓮ **kogata hōsōbutsu:** The advantages of the small packet: it travels faster (since it goes with the regular mail), and the postage rate is often cheaper than for regular packages. The weight limit is usually 1000 grams, and the packet must *not* be sealed (with tape, although string may be used). Often a **nifuda** (tag 荷札) for the address is also needed. Check with the post office for exact size, weight and other limitations which vary with the destination of the packet.

ADDITIONAL WORDS:

shūnyū inshi (revenue stamps 収入印紙)

Revenue stamps are used to pay certain government fees, such as fees for an extension of immigration status.

yūbin chokin (postal savings 郵便貯金)

Postal savings are the same as savings accounts at any bank, except that the interest rate is lower. However, income tax need not be paid on any interest earned with postal savings (while it must be paid on bank savings over ¥3,000,000.)

Overseas Postal Rates (as of February 1985)

AIRMAIL			
	Asia Australia New Zealand Midway	North America Central America West Indies	Europe Africa South America Near & Middle East
Letters: Up to 10 grams	130 yen	150 yen	170 yen
Each extra 10 grams	70	90	110
Postcards:	90	100	110
Printed matter: Up to 20 grams	90	100	110
Each extra 20 grams	50	60	70
Small packets: Up to 20 grams	90	100	110
Each extra 20 grams	50	60	70
Aerogram	120	120	120

	AIRMAIL		SEAMAIL	
Parcels:	Up to 500 grams	Each extra 500 grams	Up to 1 kg	Each extra kilogram
Southeast Asia	2,200 yen	700 yen	1,700 yen	400 yen
Southwest Asia	2,500	900	1,900	400
Oceania	2,600	1,000	1,800	400
Near & Middle East	2,800	1,050	1,800	400
West Europe	2,900	1,050	2,000 [1]	450 [2]
East Europe	2,800	1,000	2,100	700
South & Central America	3,500	1,600	2,400	500
Africa	3,100	1,400	1,900	450
Philippines	1,800	500	1,450	300
United States	2,400	1,000	1,750	600
Canada	2,400	1,000	1,750	600
East Asia [3]	1,900	400	1,700	250
East Asia [4]	2,100	550	1,850	400
Republic of South Africa	3,400	1,750	2,100	350

1) Via Cape Town: 2,000/Via Siberia: 2,300
2) Via Cape Town: 450/Via Siberia: 800
3) South Korea, Hong Kong. etc.
4) Mainland China, North Korea

ADDITIONAL WORDS (cont.):

genkin kakitome fūtō
(cash registration envelope 現金書留封筒)
　A cash registration envelope must be used when sending cash through the mail.　It must also be given directly to a postal clerk, and should not be put in a mail box.
yūbin futsū kawase (postal money order 郵便普通為替)

USEFUL EXPRESSIONS:

1.　**tegami o dasu** (to mail (or to post) a letter)
　　手紙を出す.
　　Amerika made kono tegami o dashitai n desu.
　　(I want to mail these letters to America.)
　　アメリカまでこの手紙を出したいんです.

2.　**kozutsumi o okuru**
　　(to mail (or to post) a package)
　　小包を送る.
　　Kono kozutsumi o funabin de okutte kudasai.
　　(Please send this package by seamail.)
　　この小包を船便で送ってください.

3.　**hoken** (insurance)
　　保険
　　kozutsumi ni hoken o kakeru
　　(to insure a package)
　　小包に保険をかける
　　Kono kozutsumi ni hoken o kakeru to, ikura ni narimasu ka?
　　(If I insure this package, how much will it cost?)
　　この小包に保険をかけるといくらになりますか.

4.　**Sokutatsu de onegai shimasu.**
　　(Please send this by special delivery. Lit: By special delivery, please.)
　　速達でお願いします.

5.　**Hachijū-en kitte o jū-mai kudasai.**
　　(Please give me ten 80-yen stamps.)
　　80円切手を十枚ください.

DIALOG:

Jones: Kogata hōsōbutsu o dashitai n desu ga, doko desu ka?
(Where can I mail this small packet?)
小形包装物を出したいんですがどこですか.

Clerk: Hachi-ban desu.
(That is (window) number eight.)
8番です.

(At window 8)
Jones: Kono kogata hōsōbutsu wa kōkūbin de ikura desu ka?
(How much will it cost to send this packet by airmail?)
この小形包装物は航空便でいくらですか.

Clerk: Gohyaku-guramu desu kara, sen-nihyaku-hachijū-en ni narimasu.
(This is 500 grams, so it comes to ¥1,280.)
500グラムですから1,280円になります.

Jones: Funabin de wa?
(By seamail?)
船便では.

Clerk: Hyaku-nanajū-en desu.
(That's ¥170.)
170円です.

Jones: Funabin de onegai shimasu.
(Please send it by seamail.)
船便でお願いします.

Rural **posuto**
(Mail box, see ❷)

10 At the Bank

❶ **gi-n-kō** (bank)
ぎんこう／銀行

❷ **o-ka-ne** (money)
おかね／お金

③ **[jū]-e-n da-ma** ([ten] yen coin)
[じゅう]えんだま／[10]円玉

④ **[se-n-]e-n sa-tsu** ([one thousand] yen bill)
[せん]えんさつ／[千]円札

⑤ **ge-n-ki-n** (cash)
げんきん／現金

❻ **ryo-kō-sha ko-gi-tte** (traveler's checks)
りょこうしゃこぎって／旅行者小切手

⑦ **kō-ni-n ryō-ga-e-shō** (authorized moneychanger)
こうにんりょうがえしょう／公認両替商

❽ **ka-n-sa-n ri-tsu** (exchange rate)
かんさんりつ／換算率

⑨ **e-n** (yen)
えん／円

⑩ **ma-ru-ku** (mark)
マルク

❶ **po-n-do** (pound)
ポンド

⑫ **do-ru** (dollar)
ドル

⑬ **yo-ki-n** (savings, deposit)
よきん／預金

❶ **fu-tsū yo-ki-n** (ordinary deposit, ordinary ⌊account)*
ふつうよきん／普通預金

❶ **te-i-ki yo-ki-n** (fixed (time) deposit)*
ていきよきん／定期預金

⑯ **tsu-mi-ta-te yo-ki-n** (installment savings)*
つみたてよきん／積立預金

⑰ **kō-za fu-ri-ka-e** (a kind of transfer account)*
こうざふりかえ／口座振替

⑱ **ri-shi** (interest)
りし／利子

⑲ **ga-i-ko-ku sō-ki-n** (remittance to foreign ⌊countries)*
がいこくそうきん／外国送金

⓴ **yo-ki-n tsū-chō** (bank book)
よきんつうちょう／預金通帳

55

NOTES:

*⑭ **futsū yokin:** With an ordinary account, money may be deposited and withdrawn at will, but the interest rate is very low.

*⑮ **teiki yokin:** With a fixed deposit, money may not be withdrawn until the end of a predetermined period of time, for example six months or one year. Neither may additional money be deposited during this period. However, the interest rate is higher than in the ordinary account, and the longer the period of time, the higher the rate becomes.

*⑯ **tsumitate yokin:** With installment savings, money may be deposited at any time, but not withdrawn until the end of a predetermined period of time. The interest rate is higher than in the ordinary account, and increases with the length of the deposit.

*⑰ **kōza furikae:** This kind of transfer account may be attached to an ordinary account in order to pay monthly bills. In Japan, where bill collectors usually come to the door, this is a very helpful service for persons who are not usually home during the day. At an individual's request, the bank will arrange for automatic payment of gas, electricity, telephone or other bills each month from his account.

*⑲ **gaikoku sōkin:** Remittance to foreign countries may be transferred by telegram or by airmail through the bank, or it may be issued to you in the form of a demand draft. This service is, of course, useful when you need to pay bills or fees overseas, or when you want to send money to relatives back home.

ADDITIONAL WORD:

tōza yokin (checking account 当座預金)

Checking accounts are rarely used in Japan as special qualifications are necessary to have one. Most Japanese have little use for a checking account since bills are usually paid to collectors who come to the door, through transfer accounts, or by presenting the bill and fee at almost any bank. (See Useful Expression 5, page 59.)

Ichiman-en satsu
(Ten thousand yen bill)

Gosen-en satsu
(Five thousand yen bill)

Sen-en satsu
(One thousand yen bill)

Gohyaku-en satsu
(Five hundred yen bill)

Gohyaku-en dama
(Five hundred yen coin)

Hyaku-en dama (One hundred yen coin)

Gojū-en dama (Fifty yen coin)

Jū-en dama (Ten yen coin)

Go-en dama (Five yen coin)

Ichi-en dama (One yen coin)

USEFUL EXPRESSIONS:

1. **ryōgae suru** (to exchange, to change money)
   両替する
   En ni ryōgae shite kudasai.
   (Please change (this) into yen.)
   円に両替してください.
2. **Komakaku shite kudasai.**
   (Please give me small change (for this bill).)
   こまかくしてください.
3. **Futsū yokin o hajimetai n desu ga.**
   (I want to start an ordinary savings account.)
   普通預金を始めたいんですが.
4. **orosu** (to withdraw) おろす
   Sanman-en oroshitai n desu.
   (I would like to withdraw ¥30,000.)
   三万円おろしたいんです.
5. **ryōkin** (charge, fee) 料金
   Gasu ryōkin o haraitai n desu ga, doko desu ka?
   (Where can I pay my gas bill?)
   ガス料金を払いたいんですがどこですか.

DIALOG:

Jones: **Doru ni ryōgae shite kudasai.**
(Please change (this yen) into dollars.)
ドルに両替してください.

Clerk: **Genkin ga ii desu ka, ryokōsha kogitte ga ii desu ka?**
(Would you like this in cash or traveler's checks?)
現金がいいですか. 旅行者小切手がいいですか.

Jones: **Nihyaku-doru wa ryokōsha kogitte ni, nokori wa genkin de onegai shimasu.**
(Please give me $200 in traveler's checks and the rest in cash.)
二百ドルは旅行者小切手に, のこりは現金でお願いします.

Clerk: **Shōshō omachi kudasai.**
(Please wait a moment.)
少々お待ちください.

11 Making Appointments

① **ya-ku-so-ku** (appointment)
やくそく／約束

② **i-chi-ji** (one o'clock)
いちじ／1時

❸ **i-chi-ji jū-go-fu-n** (one fifteen)
いちじじゅうごふん／1時15分

④ **i-chi-ji ha-n** (one thirty)
いちじはん／1時半

⑤ **i-chi-ji yo-n-jū-go-fu-n** (one forty-five)
いちじよんじゅうごふん／1時45分

❻ **ge-tsu-yō-bi** (Monday)
げつようび／月曜日

❼ **ro-ku-ga-tsu** (June)
ろくがつ／六月

❽ **tsu-i-ta-chi** (first)
ついたち／一日

⑨ **a-sa** (morning)
あさ／朝

⑩ **go-go** (afternoon)
ごご／午後

⑪ **yū-ga-ta** (evening)
ゆうがた／夕方

⑫ **yo-ru** (night)
よる／夜

❸ **de-n-wa** (telephone)
でんわ／電話

⑭ **kō-shū de-n-wa** (public telephone)*
こうしゅうでんわ／公衆電話

❺ **de-n-wa ba-n-gō** (telephone number)
でんわばんごう／電話番号

❻ **de-n-wa-chō** (telephone directory)
でんわちょう／電話帳

⑰ **chō-kyo-ri de-n-wa** (long distance telephone)
ちょうきょりでんわ／長距離電話

⑱ **shi-na-i de-n-wa** (local telephone)
しないでんわ／市内電話

❾ **de-n-pō** (telegram)
でんぽう／電報

⑳ **ko-ku-sa-i de-n-wa** (international telephone)*
こくさいでんわ／国際電話

NOTES:

*⑭ **kōshū denwa:** To use a public telephone, you simply pick up the receiver, drop in one or more 10-yen coins, and dial your number. Local calls are 10 yen for three minutes, but you may extend the call by dropping in more coins. For long distance calls, you must insert coins faster, depending on the distance of the call. Pay telephones will handle up to six coins at the same time, and extra coins beyond the toll charge will be returned automatically at the end of the call.

Blue telephones (in booths) are good for any distance. Tall red phones are also good for long distances, but short red phones are for local calls only. Yellow telephones accept 100-yen coins and are, therefore, especially good for long distance calls.

Short and tall **kōshū denwa** (Public telephones, see ⑭)

*⑳ **kokusai denwa:** International calls are handled by the Kokusai Denshin Denwa Co., Ltd. Overseas calls to most parts of the world may be placed in English by dialing 0051 (in Tokyo) or 03-211-5511 from all other areas of Japan. Rates vary greatly according to the time of day and the distance of the call. Call the **K.D.D.** for more information at (03) 270-5111.

TIME:

ichi-ji	(1 o'clock)	一時
ni-ji	(2 oclock)	二時
san-ji	(3 o'clock)	三時
yo-ji	(4 o'clock)	四時
go-ji	(5 o'clock)	五時
roku-ji	(6 o'clock)	六時
shichi-ji	(7 o'clock)	七時
hachi-ji	(8 o'clock)	八時
ku-ji	(9 o'clock)	九時
jū-ji	(10 o'clock)	十時
jūichi-ji	(11 o'clock)	十一時
jūni-ji	(12 o'clock)	十二時
ippun	(1 minute)	一分
ni-fun	(2 minutes)	二分
san-pun	(3 minutes)	三分
yon-pun	(4 minutes)	四分
go-fun	(5 minutes)	五分
roppun	(6 minutes)	六分
shichi-fun	(7 minutes)	七分
hachi-fun	(8 minutes)	八分
kyū-fun	(9 minutes)	九分
juppun	(10 minutes)	十分

Mae (Before 前)   Sugi (After 過ぎ)

Han (Half past 半)

DAYS OF THE WEEK:

getsu-yōbi	(Monday)	月曜日
ka-yōbi	(Tuesday)	火曜日
sui-yōbi	(Wednesday)	水曜日
moku-yōbi	(Thursday)	木曜日
kin-yōbi	(Friday)	金曜日
do-yōbi	(Saturday)	土曜日
nichi-yōbi	(Sunday)	日曜日

DAYS OF THE MONTH:

tsuitachi	(first)	ついたち
futsuka	(second)	二日
mikka	(third)	三日
yokka	(fourth)	四日
itsuka	(fifth)	五日
muika	(sixth)	六日
nanoka	(seventh)	七日
yōka	(eighth)	八日
kokonoka	(ninth)	九日
tōka	(tenth)	十日
jūichi-nichi	(eleventh)	十一日

(all the rest of the days use *-nichi* except:)

jūyokka	(fourteenth)	十四日
hatsuka	(twentieth)	二十日
nijūyokka	(twenth-fourth)	二十四日

MONTHS OF THE YEAR:

ichi-gatsu	(January)	一月
ni-gatsu	(February)	二月
san-gatsu	(March)	三月
shi-gatsu	(April)	四月
go-gatsu	(May)	五月
roku-gatsu	(June)	六月
shichi-gatsu	(July)	七月
hachi-gatsu	(August)	八月
ku-gatsu	(September)	九月
jū-gatsu	(October)	十月
jūichi-gatsu	(November)	十一月
jūni-gatsu	(December)	十二月

SEASONS OF THE YEAR:

haru	(spring)	春
natsu	(summer)	夏
aki	(autumn)	秋
fuyu	(winter)	冬

USEFUL EXPRESSIONS:

1.-ji (time, o'clock) 時
  Ima nanji desu ka? (What time is it?)
    いま何時ですか.
  [Ichi]-ji desu. (It's [one] o'clock.)
    [一] 時です.
2. **jikan** (hour) 時間
  Nanjikan kakarimasu ka?
  (How many hours will it take?)
    何時間かかりますか.
  Ichi-jikan kakarimasu.
  (It will take one hour.)
    一時間かかります.
3. **Nanyōbi desu ka?**
  (What day of the week is it?)
    何曜日ですか.
4. **Otanjōbi wa nangatsu, nannichi desu ka?**
  (What month and what day is your birthday?)
    お誕生日は何月何日ですか.
5. **Itsu aimashō ka?**
  (When shall we meet?)
    いつ会いましょうか.

OTHER TIME EXPRESSIONS:

kyō	(today)	きょう
kinō	(yesterday)	きのう
ototoi	(day before yesterday)	おととい
ashita	(tomorrow)	あした
asatte	(day after tomorrow)	あさって
kesa	(this morning)	けさ
konban	(this evening)	今晩
sengetsu	(last month)	先月
senshū	(last week)	先週
kyonen	(last year)	去年
raigetsu	(next month)	来月
raishū	(next week)	来週
rainen	(next year)	来年

65

DIALOG:

(Talking on the phone)

Jones: **Moshi moshi.**
(calling) (Hello.)
       もしもし

Tanaka: **Moshi moshi.**
       (Hello.)
       もしもし

Jones: **Tanaka-san no otaku desu ka?**
       (Is this the Tanaka residence?)
       田中さんのお宅ですか.

Tanaka: **Hai, sō desu.**
       (Yes, it is.)
       はい, そうです.

Jones: **Watakushi wa Jōnzu desu ga, Jun'ichi-san irasshaimasu ka.**
       (This is Mr. Jones. Is Jun'ichi there?)
       私はジョーンズですが, 純一さんいらっしゃいますか.

Tanaka: **Yā, Jōnzu-san. Boku desu. Konnichiwa.**
       (Oh, Mr. Jones. It's me. Good afternoon.)
       やあジョーンズさん. ぼくです. こんにちは.

Jones: **Ashita ohima desu ka?**
       (Are you free tomorrow?)
       あしたお暇ですか.

Tanaka: **Nichiyō da kara, ichinichijū hima desu.**
       (That's Sunday, so I am free all day.)
       日曜だから一日中暇です.

Jones: **Shibuya e "Sensō to Heiwa" to iu eiga o mi ni ikimasen ka?**
       (Would you like to go see the movie "War and Peace" in Shibuya?)
       渋谷へ「戦争と平和」という映画を見に行きませんか.

Tanaka: **Ii desu nē. Nanji ni, doko de aimashō ka?**
       (That sounds great. What time and where shall we meet?)
       いいですねえ. 何時にどこで会いましょうか.

Jones: **Roku-ji jūgo-fun mae ni, Hachikō no mae de wa dō desu ka?**
(How about at a quarter to six, in front of Hachiko?)
六時十五分前にハチ公の前ではどうですか.

Tanaka: **Ii desu yo.**
(That's fine.)
いいですよ.

Jones: **Jā, ashita. Sayonara.**
(Tomorrow then.   Good-by.)
じゃああした. さよなら.

Tanaka: **Sayonara.**
(Good-by.)
さよなら.

Hachikō: Hachikō (ハチ公), a statue of a dog, has become a famous and popular meeting place for the Japanese. The story of Hachi (*ko* was added later as a term of endearment) is one of unusual faithfulness even for a dog. Given to a Tokyo University professor in 1923, Hachi would follow his master to Shibuya station each morning and come to meet him again in the evening when he returned from the university. Then, in 1925, the professor suddenly died. But Hachi continued to make the trip to the station each day, waiting for his master until the streets were dark and deserted. People say that Hachi could be found waiting at the station every day for the next ten years until he died in 1935. Shortly after a statue was dedicated in his honor. Today, Hachikō reminds everyone to wait patiently.

Hachikō's statue
in Shibuya

12 Souvenirs

① **(o-)mi-ya-ge** (souvenir, present)*
（お）みやげ／（お）土産

② **mi-n-ge-i-hi-n** (folk craft, folk art)
みんげいひん／民芸品

❸ **ni-n-gyō** (doll)
にんぎょう／人形

❹ **ko-ke-shi** (*kokeshi* doll)
こけし

⑤ **nu-ri-mo-no** (lacquer ware)*
ぬりもの／塗物

❻ **fū-ri-n** (wind-bell)
ふうりん／風鈴

❼ **se-n-su** (folding fan)
せんす／扇子

⑧ **u-chi-wa** (fan)
うちわ／団扇

❾ **ka-ra-ka-sa** (Japanese umbrella)
からかさ／から傘

⑩ **hi-ga-sa** (parasol)
ひがさ／日傘

⓫ **te-ma-ri** (hand ball)
てまり／手鞠

⓬ **chō-chi-n** (lantern)
ちょうちん／提灯

⓭ **da-ru-ma** (*daruma* doll)*
だるま／達磨

⓮ **ka-ta-na** (sword)
かたな／刀

⑮ **to-ke-i** (watch)
とけい／時計

⓰ **ka-me-ra** (camera)
カメラ

⑰ **shi-n-ju** (pearl)
しんじゅ／真珠

⑱ **de-n-ki ki-gu** (electric appliances)*
でんききぐ／電機器具

⑲ **ne-bi-ki** (discount, reduction)
ねびき／値引き

⑳ **me-n-ze-i** (no tax)
めんぜい／免税

NOTES:

*❶ **omiyage:** Although *omiyage* is often translated as "souvenir," it is best to think of *omiyage* as a "present" which is given to someone else. That is, Japanese travelers will buy *omiyage* for family and friends back home, not for themselves, and visitors will take a gift (*omiyage*) to their host or hostess. However, shops that specialize in *omiyage* often have items that make good souvenirs or mementos of your trip to Japan.

*❺ **nurimono:** The ancient art and techniques of lacquer ware are practiced in several parts of Japan still today. Common items include various boxes, bowls, jars, and small tables. Two of the most usual designs used are **kachō** (flowers and birds 花鳥), and **fūgetsu** (natural scenes, lit: wind and moon 風月), which are then covered by several coats of **urushi** (lacquer 漆). Popular brands of nurimono include Aizu-nuri, Kuro-e-nuri, Wajima-nuri, Tsugaru-nuri, Noshiro-Shunkei-nuri, and Hida-Shunkei-nuri.

*❽ **daruma:** The *daruma* doll is sold today as a good-luck charm, but its origin may be traced to a Buddhist figure known as Bodhidharma, an Indian who traveled to China in the sixth century. Legend says that he sat for so long in the *zen* posture while searching for the Buddha that he "lost" his legs and arms. Therefore, he is now represented as a doll shaped without any limbs so that it will always return to an upright position when knocked over. This "persevering" feature of the *daruma* doll lends to the belief that it is good luck and will bring success. After purchasing one of these dolls, the owner will paint in one of its eyes (which are blank at first) while hoping for success in some endeavor. When success is achieved, the other eye is also painted in.

*⑱ denki kigu: In Akihabara, a section of Tokyo, electrical appliances are sold at significantly reduced prices. Moreover, shops regularly sell below the discount prices marked on their merchandise. A little charm and a bit of persuasion can help you get a favorable deal on your purchase of electric appliances in Akihabara.

ADDITIONAL WORDS:

furoshiki (wrapping cloth 風呂敷)

Some *furoshiki* are so artfully designed that many foreigners use them as table cloths or wall-hangings. Japanese have traditionally used them to carry things.

byōbu (folding screens 屏風)

soroban (abacus 算盤)

origami (folded paper 折紙)

Origami is a kind of an art in which paper is folded to make the shape of various animals or objects, such as a crane (the bird) or a turtle. (See also page 113.)

irogami (colored paper 色紙)

Irogami is used in *origami*.

takezaiku (bamboo-wear 竹細工)

takefūrin (bamboo wind-bell 竹風鈴)

Furoshiki (Wrapping cloth)

Origami (Folded paper)

Akihabara, a good place to purchase **denki kigu** (electric appliances, see ⑱)

USEFUL EXPRESSIONS:

1. **sābisu sentā** (service center)

   サービスセンター

   [Amerika] ni [Sonii] no sābisu sentā ga arimasu ka?

   (Is there a service center for [Sony] in [America]?)

   アメリカにソニーのサービスセンターがありますか.

2. **haitatsu** (delivery)

   配達

   Hoteru made haitatsu shite moraemasu ka?

   (Can I have it delivered to my hotel?)

   ホテルまで配達してもらえますか.

3. **[Amerika] made okutte moraemasu ka?**

   (Can I have it mailed to [America]?)

   アメリカまで送ってもらえますか.

4. **setsumeisho** (explanation, explanatory note)

   説明書

   Eigo no setsumeisho wa arimasu ka?

   (Do you have a (written) explanation in English?)

   英語の説明書はありますか.

DIALOG:

(At Akihabara)

Jones: **Kono rajio wa ikura desu ka?**

(How much is this radio?)

このラジオはいくらですか.

Clerk: **Sore wa gosen-en desu.**

(That's ¥5,000.)

それは五千円です.

Jones: **Motto yasui no wa arimasen ka?**

(Don't you have a cheaper one?)

もっと安いのはありませんか.

Clerk: **Sō desu nē. Kore wa ikaga desu ka? Yonsen-en desu.**

(Let's see. How about this one? It's ¥4,000.)

そうですねえ. これはいかがですか. 四千円です.

Jones: **Ii desu ga, sukoshi yasuku dekimasen ka?**

(That's better, but can't you make it a little cheaper?)

いいですが, すこし安くできませんか.

Clerk: **Sanzen-nanahyaku-en dewa ikaga desu ka?**

(How about (a discount to) ¥3,700?)

三千七百円ではいかがですか.

Jones: **Dewa, kore o moraimashō.**

(Then, I'll take it.)

ではこれをもらいましょう.

13 Shops and Shopping

① **ka-i-mo-no** (shopping)
かいもの／買物

❷ **ni-ku-ya** (butcher)
にくや／肉屋

❸ **ya-o-ya** (vegetable store)
やおや／八百屋

❹ **ku-da-mo-no(-ya)** (fruit (store))
くだもの(や)／果物(屋)

⑤ **pa-n-ya** (bakery)
パンや／パン屋

⑥ **sa-ka-ya** (liquor store)
さかや／酒屋

⑦ **sū-pā-mā-ke-tto** (supermarket)
スーパーマーケット

⑧ **(o-)ka-shi(-ya)** (candy (store))
(お)かし(や)／(お)菓子(屋)

⑨ **de-pā-to** (department store)
デパート

⑩ **ko-ttō(-ten)** (curio (shop))
こっとう(てん)／骨董(店)

⑪ **se-to-mo-no(-ya)** (chinaware (store))
せともの(や)／瀬戸物(屋)

⑫ **o-mo-cha(-ya)** (toy (store))
おもちゃ(や)／玩具(屋)

⑬ **ka-me-ra(-ya)** (camera (shop))
カメラ(や)／カメラ(屋)

⑭ **bu-n-bō-gu(-ya)** (stationery (store))
ぶんぼうぐ(や)／文房具(屋)

⑮ **ho-n(-ya)** (book (store))
ほん(や)／本(屋)

⑯ **fu-ru-ho-n(-ya)** (used book (store))*
ふるほん(や)／古本(屋)

⑰ **ka-gu(-ya)** (furniture (store))
かぐ(や)／家具(屋)

⑱ **go-fu-ku(-ya)** (*kimono*-cloth (shop))
ごふく(や)／呉服(屋)

❶❾ **te-n-i-n** (salesclerk)
てんいん／店員

⑳ **(o-)tsu-ri** (change)
(お)つり／(お)釣

NOTES:

* furuhon-ya: A great number of used bookstores can be found in the Kanda, Hongo, and Waseda areas of Tokyo.　There are plenty of books in English and other languages besides Japanese.　A map of these areas is available from the International House of Japan, 11-16, 5-chome, Roppongi, Minato-ku, Tokyo (tel: 401-9151).

Furuhon-ya (Used bookstore, see ⓰) in the Kanda area

ADDITIONAL WORDS:

niku (meat 肉)
    gyūniku (beef 牛肉)
    butaniku (pork 豚肉)
    toriniku (chicken 鶏肉)
yasai (vegetable 野菜)
    tamanegi (round onion 玉ねぎ)
    naganegi (leek 長ねぎ)
    ingen (string beans 隠元)
    ninjin (carrot 人参)
    kyabetsu (cabbage キャベツ)
    retasu (lettuce レタス)
    daikon (radish 大根)
    jagaimo (potato 馬鈴薯)
kudamono (fruit 果物)
    mikan (tangerine 蜜柑)
    nashi (Japanese pear 梨)
    momo (peach 桃)
    ichigo (strawberry いちご)
    budō (grape 葡萄)
    ringo (apple 林檎)
    suika (watermelon 西瓜)
pan (bread パン)

enpitsu (pencil 鉛筆)
bōru pen (ball point pen ボールペン)
kami (paper 紙)

takai (expensive 高い)
yasui (cheap 安い)

ōkii (big 大きい)
chiisai (small 小さい)

sukoshi (a little 少し)
takusan (much, many たくさん)

ii (good いい)
kirei (beautiful きれい)
oishii (delicious おいしい)

USEFUL EXPRESSIONS:

1. **Kono hen ni [kudamono-ya] wa arimasu ka?**
   (Is there a [fruit shop] in this area?)
   このへんに [果物屋] はありますか.
2. **are** (that over there)
   あれ
   Are o misete kudasai.
   (Please show me that.)
   あれを見せてください.
3. **Ikura desu ka?** (How much is it?)
   いくらですか.
4. **kore** (this)
   これ
   Kore o mittsu kudasai.
   (Please give me three of these.)
   これを三つください.
5. **Motto ōkii no wa arimasen ka?**
   (Don't you have a bigger one?)
   もっと大きいのはありませんか.

DIALOGS:

(At a fruit shop)

Jones: **Are wa nan desu ka?**
(What are those?)
あれは何ですか.

Clerk: **Kore desu ka?**
(Do you mean these?)
これですか.

Jones: **Hai, sore desu.**
(Yes, those.)
はい, それです.

Clerk: **Kore wa nashi desu.   Oishii desu yo.**
(These are (Japanese) pears.   They are delicious.)
これは梨です. おいしいですよ.

Jones: **Jā, hito-yama kudasai.**
(Well, give me one bunch, please.)
じゃあ. 一山ください.

(At the information booth in a department store)

Jones: **Omocha wa doko desu ka?**

(Where are the toys?)

おもちゃはどこですか.

Clerk: **Go-kai de gozaimasu.**

(They are on the fifth floor.)

五階でございます.

TABLE OF WEIGHTS AND MEASURES

WEIGHTS:

1 pound	454 **guramu** (grams グラム)
1 ounce	28 grams
3-1/2 oz.	100 grams
2 lb. 3 oz.	⎰ 1000 grams ⎱ 1 **kiro** (kilogram キロ)

LENGTHS:

1 mile	1.6 **kiro** (kilometer キロ)
1 yard	⎰ 0.91 **mētoru** (meter メートル) ⎱ 91 **senchi** (centimeter センチ)
1 foot	30 centimeters
1 inch	2.54 centimeters
3/8 inch	1 centimeter
39-3/8 inch	1 meter
0.62 mile	1 kilometer

LIQUIDS:

1 quart	0.95 **rittoru** (liter リットル)
1 pint	⎰ 0.47 liter ⎱ 470 **shiishii** (cubic centimeters, c.c.)
1.06 quart	1 liter
1.05 gallon	4 liters

① **o-n-ga-ku-ka-i** (music concert)*
　　おんがくかい／音楽会
② **o-pe-ra** (opera)
　　オペラ
③ **ge-ki, shi-ba-i** (play, drama)
　　げき／劇，しばい／芝居
④ **ge-ki-jō** (theater)
　　げきじょう／劇場
❺ **e-i-ga** (movie)*
　　えいが／映画
❻ **e-i-ga-ka-n** (movie theater)
　　えいがかん／映画館
⑦ **ka-i-jō ji-ka-n** (opening time)
　　かいじょうじかん／開場時間
❽ **ki-ppu u-ri-ba** (box office)
　　きっぷうりば／切符売場
⑨ **yo-ya-ku** (reservation)
　　よやく／予約
⑩ **ma-e-u-ri ki-ppu** (advanced ticket)
　　まえうりきっぷ／前売切符
❶ **za-se-ki** (seat)
　　ざせき／座席
⑫ **shi-te-i-se-ki** (reserved seat)
　　していせき／指定席
⑬ **ta-chi-mi-se-ki** (standing room)
　　たちみせき／立見席
❹ **pu-ro-gu-ra-mu** (program)
　　プログラム
⑮ **pu-re-i ga-i-do** (Play Guide)*
　　プレイガイド
⑯ **kya-ba-rē** (cabaret)*
　　キャバレー
⑰ **bā** (bar)*
　　バー
⑱ **na-i-to ku-ra-bu** (nightclub)*
　　ナイトクラブ
⑲ **ho-su-te-su** (hostess)*
　　ホステス
⑳ **se-ki-ryō** (cover charge)
　　せきりょう／席料

NOTES:

***❶** **ongakukai:** Concerts (as well as plays and movies) are given considerable coverage in the English-language newspapers of Japan.

***❺** **eiga:** In Japan, foreign movies are about as popular as domestic films, despite some great work by Japanese filmmakers including the much acclaimed Ozu, Mizoguchi, and Kurosawa. Among the popular types of Japanese films today are the **yakuza** (gangster やくざ) films which have a great following and the **jidaigeki** (period pieces 時代劇) variety which includes the exciting **chanbara** (sword battles ちゃんばら) of the *samurai* and which are most commonly found on TV replays.

First-run movies are called **rōdoshō** (roadshows ロードショウ) in Japan. If you attend a first-run movie on a Sunday or holiday, you should be prepared to stand. Tickets are sold as long as people will buy them, whether there are seats available or not.

***⓯** **purei gaido:** Play Guides handle ticket sales for most major entertainment including concerts, plays, movies, and sports. Play Guides are located conveniently in many department stores and other central locations.

Yakuza (Gangster, see note **❺**) as played by actor Ken Takakura
Picture courtesy of Toei Movie Company

Picture courtesy of Toei Movie Company

Chanbara (Sword battle, see note **5**)

16 **kyabarei:** Cabarets are those night spots which have hostesses, a dance band, and often a floor show as well. Japanese cabarets and other night spots tend to be rather expensive, expecially in the Ginza, Akasaka, and Roppongi areas. Most of their patrons are businessmen entertaining important guests at company expense; private individuals on a modest income will rarely walk into such places.

17 **bā:** Bars do not usually employ hostesses; drinking is the main order of business.

18 **naito kurabu:** Nightclubs have hostesses for their patrons, but there is no dancing, and many clubs are for members only.

19 **hosutesu:** Hostesses, of course, attempt to please the customer through conversation, dancing and other services, but the customer pays (often handsomely) for this service by the hour, by the drink, or by both the hour and the drink.

ADDITIONAL WORDS:

sutorippu shō (striptease ストリップショー)
nūdo (nude ヌード)
poruno (porno ポルノ)
pinku eiga (pink movie, pornographic movie ピンク映画)

USEFUL EXPRESSIONS:

1. **kaien jikan** (starting time)
   開演時間
   Kaien jikan o oshiete kudasai.
   (Please tell me the starting times (of the shows).)
   開演時間を教えてください.
2. **suwaru** (to sit down)
   座る
   Ima suwaremasu ka.
   (Can we sit down now?　(That is, "Are there vacant seats?"))
   いま座れますか.
3. **Kono eiga wa itsu made desu ka?**
   (Until when will this movie be (showing)?)
   この映画はいつまでですか.

Purei Gaido (Play Guide, see ⑮)

84

DIALOG:

Jones: **Eiga e ikimasen ka?**
(Would you like to go to a movie?)
映画へ行きませんか.

Tanaka: **Ii desu nē. Donna eiga desu ka?**
(That sounds good. What kind of movie is it?)
いいですねえ. どんな映画ですか.

Jones: **"Tokyo Monogatari" to iu, yūmei na Nihon no eiga desu.**
(It is a famous Japanese movie called "Tokyo Story.")
「東京物語」という有名な日本の映画です.

Tanaka: **Ii eiga da sō desu ne. Mae kara mitai to omotte imashita.**
(I've heard that's a good movie. I've been thinking for a long time that I want to see it.)
いい映画だそうですね. 前から見たいと思っていました.

Jones: **Nihongo ga mada yoku wakaranai kara, wakaranai tokoro wa ato de setsumei shite kuremasen ka?**
(Since I still don't speak Japanese so well, would you please explain the parts I don't understand later?)
日本語がまだよく分らないから, 分らないところは, あとで説明してくれませんか.

Tanaka: **Hai. Muzukashii kamo shiremasen ga, yatte mimashō.**
(Certainly. It'll probably be difficult, but I'll try.)
はい. 難しいかもしれませんがやってみましょう.

15 At the Doctor's

① **byō-ki** (illness, sickness)
びょうき／病気

❷ **byō-i-n** (hospital)
びょういん／病院

❸ **(o-)i-sha(-sa-n)** (doctor)
（お）いしゃ（さん）／（お）医者（さん）

④ **ha-i-sha(-sa-n)** (dentist)
はいしゃ（さん）／歯医者（さん）

❺ **ka-n-go-fu(-sa-n)** (nurse)
かんごふ（さん）／看護婦（さん）

❻ **chū-sha** (injection, shot)
ちゅうしゃ／注射

⑦ **sho-hō-se-n** (prescription)
しょほうせん／処方箋

⑧ **te-n-ne-n-tō** (smallpox)
てんねんとう／天然痘

⑨ **ka-ra-da** (body)
からだ／体

❿ **a-ta-ma** (head)
あたま／頭

⓫ **me** (eye)
め／目

⓬ **ha-na** (nose)
はな／鼻

⓭ **mi-mi** (ear)
みみ／耳

⓮ **ku-chi** (mouth)
くち／口

⑮ **ha** (tooth)
は／歯

⑯ **ku-bi** (neck)
くび／首

⓱ **u-de** (arm)
うで／腕

⓲ **te** (hand)
て／手

⑲ **yu-bi** (finger)
ゆび／指

⓴ **a-shi** (leg, foot)
あし／足

USEFUL EXPRESSIONS:

1. **itai** (to hurt, to be sore) 痛い
   Mimi ga itai desu.
   (My ear hurts.)
   　　耳が痛いです.
   Ashi ga itai desu.
   (I have a sore leg.)
   　　足が痛いです.
   Koko ga itai desu.
   (I have a pain here.)
   　　ここが痛いです.
   Atama ga tottemo itai desu.
   (I have a terrible headache.)
   　　頭がとっても痛いです.

2. **hakike** (nausea)
   　　吐き気
   Hakike ga shimasu.
   (I have nausea.)
   　　吐き気がします.

3. **kimochi** (feeling) 気持
   Kimochi ga warui desu.
   (I feel sick to the stomach.)
   　　気持が悪いです.

4. **darui** (tired, languid) だるい
   Karada ga darui desu.
   (My whole body feels tired.)
   　　体がだるいです.

5. **kenkō shindan** (physical examination)
   　　健康診断
   Kenkō shindan shite kudasai.
   (Please give me a physical examination.)
   　　健康診断してください.

6. **Yoyaku o onegaishimasu.**
   (I'd like to make an appointment (to see the doctor).)
   　　予約をお願いします.

7. **yobō chūsha** (preventative injection, immunization)
   　　予防注射
   Tennentō no yobō chūsha o shite kudasai.
   (Please give me a smallpox vaccination.)
   　　天然痘の予防注射をしてください.

ILLNESSES:

korera (cholera コレラ)
gan (cancer ガン)
shinzōbyō (heart disease 心臓病)
ikaiyō (ulcer 胃潰瘍)
shōnimahi (polio 小児マヒ)
haien (pneumonia 肺炎)
seibyō (venereal disease 性病)
mōchōen (appendicitis 盲腸炎)
chifusu (typhoid fever チフス)
haibyō (tuberculosis 肺病)
arerugii (alergy アレルギー)

OTHER PARTS OF THE BODY:

i (stomach 胃)
onaka, hara (abdomen お腹, 腹)
shinzō (heart 心臓)
hai (lungs 肺)
nodo (throat 喉)
kanzō (liver 肝臓)
chō (intestines 腸)
senaka (back 背中)
hiza (knee 膝)
hiji (elbow ひじ)
kata (shoulder 肩)
shita (tongue 舌)

MEDICAL TERMS:

ketsuatsu (blood pressure 血圧)
kōketsuatsu (high blood pressure 高血圧)
teiketsuatsu (low blood pressure 低血圧)
taion (body temperature 体温)
myakuhaku (pulse 脈拍)
shujutsu (operation 手術)
rentogen (x-ray レントゲン)

❶ **ku-su-ri-ya** (drugstore)
くすりや／薬屋

② **ku-su-ri** (medicine)
くすり／薬

❸ **ka-ze-gu-su-ri** (cold medicine)
かぜぐすり／風邪薬

④ **se-ki no ku-su-ri** (cough medicine)
せきのくすり／咳の薬

⑤ **me-gu-su-ri** (eye drops)
めぐすり／目薬

⑥ **a-su-pi-ri-n** (aspirin)
アスピリン

❼ **bi-ta-mi-n-za-i** (vitamin pill)
ビタミンざい／ビタミン剤

⑧ **ka-ze** (cold)
かぜ／風邪

⑨ **ne-tsu** (fever)
ねつ／熱

⑩ **se-ki** (cough)
せき／咳

⑪ **ku-sha-mi** (sneeze)
くしゃみ

⓬ **ta-i-o-n-ke-i** (thermometer)
たいおんけい／体温計

❸ **hō-ta-i** (bandage)
ほうたい／包帯

⑭ **gā-ze** (gauze)
ガーゼ

⑮ **ba-n-do-e-i-do** (band-Aid)
バンド・エイド

⑯ **a-ru-kō-ru** (alcohol)
アルコール

⑰ **da-sshi-me-n** (absorbent cotton)
だっしめん／脱脂綿

⓲ **ba-n-sō-kō** (adhesive tape)
ばんそうこう／絆創膏

⓳ **ha-bu-ra-shi** (toothbrush)
はブラシ／歯ブラシ

⓴ **ne-ri-ha-mi-ga-ki** (toothpaste)
ねりはみがき／煉り歯磨

USEFUL EXPRESSIONS:

1. **kayui** (to itch)
   かゆい
   Me ga kayui desu.
   (My eye itches.)
   目がかゆいです.
2. **Netsu ga arimasu ka?**
   (Do you have a fever?)
   熱がありますか.
3. **Kaze o hikimashita.**
   (I caught a cold.)
   風邪をひきました.
4. **Hana ga deru n desu.**
   (My nose is running.)
   はながでるんです.
5. **Seki ga tomaranai n desu.**
   (I can't stop coughing.)
   咳が止まらないんです.
6. **Kata ga koru n desu.**
   (My shoulders are stiff.)
   肩が凝るんです.

ADDITIONAL WORDS:

yakkyoku (pharmacy 薬局)
keshōhin (cosmetics 化粧品)
heyā burashi (hair brush ヘヤーブラシ)
kushi (comb 櫛)
tsumekiri (nail clippers 爪切り)
kamisori (razor 剃刀)

Part Two
Only in Japan

17 Tea Ceremony and Flower Arrangement

① **sa-dō, cha-no-yu** (tea ceremony)*
　　さどう／茶道，ちゃのゆ／茶の湯

❷ **cha-shi-tsu** (tea house, tea room)*
　　ちゃしつ／茶室

③ **ma-tcha** (powdered green tea)*
　　まっちゃ／抹茶

❹ **ka-ma** (hot water kettle)*
　　かま／釜

❺ **cha-i-re** (tea caddy, tea canister)*
　　ちゃいれ／茶入れ

❻ **cha-wa-n** (ceremonial tea bowl)*
　　ちゃわん／茶碗

❼ **cha-se-n** (split bamboo tea whisk)*
　　ちゃせん／茶筅

❽ **cha-sha-ku** (tea scoop)*
　　ちゃしゃく／茶杓

⑨ **ke-n-su-i** (basin for waste water)
　　けんすい／建水

⑩ **hi-sha-ku** (dipper)
　　ひしゃく／柄杓

⑪ **fu-ta-o-ki** (stand for the lid of the hot water
　　ふたおき／蓋置　　　　　⌊kettle)

⑫ **fu-ku-sa** (silk cloth for wiping dry instruments)
　　ふくさ／帛紗

⑬ **cha-ki-n** (linen cloth for wiping wet instruments)
　　ちゃきん／茶巾

⑭ **ka-i-shi** (pocket paper)*
　　かいし／懐紙

⑮ **i-ke-ba-na** (flower arrangement)*
　　いけばな／生け花

⑯ **mo-ri-ba-na** (flowers arranged in a basin)*
　　もりばな／盛花

❼ **su-i-ba-n** (basin)
　　すいばん／水盤

⑱ **ke-n-za-n** (needlepoint flower holder)
　　けんざん／剣山

⑲ **na-ge-i-re** (flower arrangement in a tall vase)*
　　なげいれ／投げ入れ

⑳ **ka-bi-n** (vase)
　　かびん／花瓶

NOTES:

*❶ **sadō, cha-no-yu:** *Sadō* literally means "the way of tea," and *cha-no-yu* means "hot water of tea," but both refer to the traditional art of the Japanese tea ceremony. Largely due to the influence of Zen Buddhism, the tea ceremony cultivates a sense of inner serenity in both the host and his guests. To participate in the tea ceremony is to be absorbed by the quiet beauty and simple elegance which accompany even the slightest detail of the ceremony. The tea master must strive for perfection of performance over many years, and even the guests, who receive tea and **wagashi** (Japanese cake 和菓子) from the master, perform in a prescribed manner which takes some time to learn. Today there are two main schools of the tea ceremony: Omote Senke and Ura Senke.

*❷ **chashitsu:** The tea house or tea room is designed especially for tea ceremony. It will contain a place in the floor for a sunken fire as well as places for an appropriate *kakejiku* or hanging scroll to be hung and for a suitable flower arrangement to be placed.

*❸ **matcha:** The powdered green tea used in the tea ceremony comes in two consistencies: **koicha** (thick tea 濃茶) and **usucha** (thin tea 薄茶). *Koicha* is shared by all guests from the same tea bowl, while *usucha* is put into individual bowls for each guest.

*❹ **kama:** The hot water kettle is put over a **ro** (sunken fire 炉) during the winter, but is placed on a **furo** (fire container 風炉) in summer months.

*❺ **chaire:** A ceramic tea caddy is called a *chaire* and is used to hold the powdered tea for *koicha*. Tea for *usucha* is put in a **natsume** (laquered tea caddy なつめ).

*❻ **chawan:** The tea bowl is an important focus of attention in the tea ceremony. It should reflect both simplicity and elegance consistent with the tea ceremony as a whole. Tea bowls are usually hand-made creations by individual craftsmen and can be quite expensive.

*❼ **chasen:** The split bamboo tea whisk is used to mix the powdered tea and water.

*❽ **chashaku:** The tea scoop is used to carry the

powdered tea from the *chaire* to the tea bowl.

*⑭ **kaishi**: Pocket paper is used by the guests to place their *wagashi* or Japanese cake on, or to wipe the tea bowl dry after they have drunk the tea.

*⑮ **ikebana**: Although flowers were certainly appreciated long before, it was not until the 15th century that flower arrangement became a distinct art in Japan. Like tea ceremony, which developed almost simultaneously, flower arrangement has been profoundly influenced by Buddhism. Today, both traditional and modern styles of flower arrangement are studied in the various schools including Ikenobo, Ohara and Sogetsu. The Ikenobo School tends to be the most traditional, while the other two have made many innovations in the art of flower arrangement.

*⑯ **moribana**: *Moribana* is a rather modern style of flower arrangement, which characteristically employs the *suiban* or basin and *kenzan* or needlepoint flower holder.

*⑲ **nageire**: *Nageire* is a traditional style of *ikebana* and is commonly used in formal tea ceremonies. Flowers in this tyle of arrangement are put into a tall vase without the use of a *kenzan*.

Cha-no-yu (Tea ceremony, see ❶) Ikebana in the **nageire** style (see ⑲)

18 Music and Dance

98

① **o-n-ga-ku** (music)
　　おんがく／音楽

② **o-do-ri** (dance)
　　おどり／踊り

③ **hō-ga-ku** (Japanese music)*
　　ほうがく／邦楽

❹ **ni-ho-n bu-yō** (Japanese dance)
　　にほんぶよう／日本舞踊

⑤ **mi-n-yō** (folk song)*
　　みんよう／民謡

❻ **mi-n-zo-ku bu-yō** (folk dance)
　　みんぞくぶよう／民族舞踊

⑦ **u-ta** (song)
　　うた／歌

⑧ **kyo-ku** (a piece, a musical selection)
　　きょく／曲

⑨ **ga-ga-ku** (ancient ceremonial court music)*
　　ががく／雅楽

⑩ **bu-ga-ku** (court dance and music)
　　ぶがく／舞楽

⑪ **ka-gu-ra** (*Shintō* music and dance)
　　かぐら／神楽

❷ **shō-myō** (Buddhist chanting)
　　しょうみょう／声明

❸ **ko-to** (Japanese "harp")*
　　こと／箏

❹ **sha-ku-ha-chi** (vertical flute)*
　　しゃくはち／尺八

❺ **sha-mi-se-n** (three-stringed guitar-like
　　しゃみせん／三味線　　　　⌊instrument)*

❻ **bi-wa** (Japanese lute)*
　　びわ／琵琶

❼ **ta-i-ko** (drum)*
　　たいこ／太鼓

❽ **ko-tsu-zu-mi** (small hand drum)*
　　こつづみ／小鼓

❾ **shō** (organ-like wind instrument)*
　　しょう／笙

⑳ **hi-chi-ri-ki** (double reed *gagaku* instrument)*
　　ひちりき

NOTES:

*❸ **hōgaku:** Japanese music and dance are not given much coverage in the English-language papers of Japan, so it is necessary to search a little to find places to see and hear these traditional Japanese arts. One place is the famous Gion Corner of Kyoto which offers the tourist a brief sampling of tea ceremony, *koto* and *shamisen* music, *geisha* dancing, *gagaku*, and *bunraku*—all in two hours. Otherwise, you may want to check your local Play Guide which should have information about major performances of Japanese music and dance.

*❺ **min'yō:** Japanese folk songs are performed nightly at **min'yō sakaba** (folk song drinking establishments 民謡 酒場) in Asakusa in Tokyo. The performers in these intimate places encourage everyone to sing along to the accompaniment of *taiko*, *shamisen*, and/or *shakuhachi*. Some customers get so caught up in the festivities that they will stand to lead a few folk songs themselves.

Min'yo sakaba (see note ❺)

*❾ **gagaku:** Literally meaning "elegant music," *gagaku* is still played today much as it was over a thousand years ago. Originally this ancient ceremonial court music was reserved for the Imperial Court and certain

100

Gagaku ensemble (see ❾)

Picture courtesy of Yoshihisa Oshida

religious ceremonies but now it may be enjoyed by everyone. For information about performances or *gagaku* itself, contact the **Nippon Gagaku Kai** (Japan Gagaku Society 日本雅楽会):

The Japan Gagaku Society	日本雅楽会
438, Minami Ōizumi-chō	東京都練馬区
Nerima-ku, Tokyo	南大泉町 438
(Tel: 922-4012)	

Bugaku (see ❿)

Picture courtesy of Yoshihisa Oshida

*⓭ **koto:** Although the word *koto* originally meant any kind of stringed instrument, it now refers to that specific instrument which is largely a product of the Edo Period, is played in a horizontal position, and usually has thirteen strings. The strings are tuned by means of **ji** (bridges 柱), but the pitches may be varied by pressing

Kagura (see ❶)   Picture courtesy of Yoshihisa Oshida

down with the left hand beyond the bridge while plucking with the right, and by other techniques. The sound of the *koto* has been described as harp-like, but it must be heard to be fully appreciated.

*⓮ shakuhachi: Usually made out of a single piece of bamboo, the *shakuhachi* is a deceptively simple instrument. Although there are only five holes, the chromatic and other scales may be produced through various fingering and blowing techniques, which take years to learn. The *shakuhachi* is an introspective instrument, which may explain its close connection with Zen Buddhism. Its plaintive but alluring sound is best appreciated in solo, although it is sometimes played with other instruments.

*⓯ shamisen: Although the *shamisen* is described as "guitar-like," it does not resemble the guitar in either playing techniques or in tonal quality. There are no frets on the long neck of the *shamisen*, and the performer must press the string at the proper point to bring forth the desired note, while his other hand plucks the string with either his finger or a **bachi** (plectrum 撥). The body of the *shamisen* is covered either by catskin or, more recently, by dog skin which is less expensive. The snap of the plectrum hitting the catskin, the twang of the lowest string, and a unique resonance combine to give the *shamisen* its beautiful, but un-Western sound. The *shamisen* may be heard in a wide variety of situations including the music accompanying *Bunraku* and *Kabuki*, as well as other folk and narrative music.

102

*⑯ biwa: The *biwa* was originally an insturment used only in *gagaku*, but long ago it was adapted to a popular form of narrative music which preserved many famous tales and legends over the centuries. Today this style of music has decreased in popularity, much like the ballad singer of the West disappeared with more modern forms of entertainment. However, some artists continue the ancient tradition by learning the *biwa* and its music. A distinctive feature of the *biwa* is the high frets which allow the strings to be depressed a great deal, thereby producing various pitches instead of a predetermined pitch such as the guitar produces.

*⑰ taiko: *Taiko* is a term used generally to mean any drum, but it especially refers to the stick drum which is used in *Nō* and in other kinds of music. A dynamic drum used in many folk festivals is the **ōdaiko** (big drum 大太鼓).

*⑱ kotsuzumi: The *kotsuzumi* is a small, hourglass-shaped drum used commonly in *Nō* and *Kabuki*. A distinctive feature of this drum is the way that the ropes which bind the heads to the body of the drum are squeezed to raise the pitch of the drum.

*⑲ shō: The *shō,* a mouth-organ with seventeen reed pipes, produces an eerily beautiful organ-like sound. It is used primarily in *gagaku*.

*⑳ hichiriki: The unique sound of the *hichiriki,* an oboe-like instrument, is either completely delightful or completely disgusting, depending on your preferences. No one seems to have a neutral position. The *hichiriki* is an important *gagaku* instrument.

Hichiriki player (see ⑳)

Picture courtesy of
Yoshihisa Oshida

103

19 Theatrical Arts

❶ **Ka-bu-ki** (*Kabuki*, Japanese traditional theater)*
かぶき／歌舞伎

❷ **ha-na-mi-chi** (flower path, a walkway through
はなみち／花道   ⌊the audience)*

❸ **mi-e** (contorted pose of *Kabuki* actor at
みえ／見得   ⌊dramatic moments)*

④ **ku-ro-ko** (stage assistant in *Kabuki*)
くろこ／黒子

⑤ **o-n-na-ga-ta, o-ya-ma** (female impersonator)*
おんながた／女形，おやま

⑥ **Nō** (*Nō*, *Nō* dance, *Nō* play, Japanese
のう／能   ⌊lyrical drama)*

⑦ **shi-te** (principal actor in *Nō*)*
シテ

⑧ **wa-ki** (supporting actor in *Nō*)
ワキ

⑨ **nō-me-n** (*Nō* mask)
のうめん／能面

⑩ **ji-u-ta-i** (*Nō* chorus)*
じうたい／地謡

⑪ **ha-ya-shi** (*Nō* ensemble)*
はやし／囃子

⑫ **ka-ga-mi no ma** (green room)*
かがみのま／鏡の間

⑬ **ha-shi-ga-ka-ri** (bridge from the green room to
はしがかり／橋掛り   ⌊the main stage)

⑭ **Kyō-ge-n** (*Nō* comedy)*
きょうげん／狂言

⑮ **Bu-n-ra-ku** (*Bunraku*, Japanese traditional
ぶんらく／文楽   ⌊puppet theater)*

⑯ **o-mo-zu-ka-i** (leader of puppeteer trio)*
おもづかい／面使い

⑰ **hi-da-ri-zu-ka-i** (second of puppeteer trio)*
ひだりづかい／左使い

⑱ **a-shi-zu-ka-i** (third of puppeteer trio)*
あしづかい／足使い

⑲ **Gi-da-yū-bu-shi** (music for *Bunraku*)*
ぎだゆうぶし／義太夫節

⑳ **Ra-ku-go** (*Rakugo*, comic story telling)*
らくご／落語

NOTES:

*❶ Kabuki: *Kabuki* was begun over 350 years ago by a woman dancer known as Okuni. Women were the only performers in her dramas which were rather sensual in presentation—and popular. In 1629 the Tokugawa Shogunate prohibited Okuni from presenting her dramas because it was felt that they were somehow corrupting public morals. Subsequently, young men began to perform these dramas, but they too met resistance from the government. It was not until adult men took over the roles that *Kabuki* began to settle into its present form. Today, *Kabuki* actors belong to certain families which have passed this dramatic tradition from father to son over the centuries.

Kabuki performances contain three or more distinct types of stories. First in order is **jidaimono** (plays dealing with historical events 時代物) and/or **aragoto** (plays in which the hero possesses superhuman characteristics 荒事). *Aragoto* are performed by the Ichikawa family and are noted for their distinctive use of **kumadori** (special make-up 隈取). *Kumadori* is applied in a unique and exaggerated fashion to reveal the nature of the character who wears it. Red colors usually indicate righteousness while indigo indicates evil. The second type of play to be staged during a *Kabuki* performance is called **buyōgeki** (dance plays 舞踊劇), and finally comes the type called **sewamono** (plays dealing with the everyday life of the common people 世話物).

Kabuki may be viewed at various theaters including the famous Kabukiza just off the Ginza in Tokyo, the New Kabukiza in Osaka, the Minamiza in Kyoto, and sometimes at the **Kokuritsu Gekijō** (National Theater 国立劇場) in Tokyo.

*❷ hanamichi: A unique feature of *Kabuki* is the "flower path" which runs from stage right, through the audience, to the rear of the auditorium. It is used for the entrance and exit of *Kabuki* actors and provides an intimate sort of contact between the actors and the audience.

*❸ **mie:** At particularly climactic moments in *Kabuki*, the actor will strike and hold a tense pose which vividly expresses his emotion.

*❺ **onnagata, oyama:** The men who play the female parts in *Kabuki* are called *onnagata* or *oyama*. They must train from childhood for their roles, and they are so successful in their impersonations that they often appear more feminine than real women.

*❻ **Nō:** *Nō*, having its origins in the 14th century, is an older art form than *Kabuki*, but still the works of one of *Nō*'s founders, Zeami Motokiyo (1363-1443), make up a large portion of the *Nō* plays performed today. *Nō* is a sophisticated combination of several stage arts: drama, dance, and both instrumental and vocal music. The audience must have an active imagination to appreciate the aesthetic nature of *Nō*; the action and other elements are largely symbolic and therefore notably less dramatic and less realistic than those of *Kabuki*.

Each performance of *Nō* traditionally consists of five parts, which consecutively deal with a god, a warrior, a woman, a mentally deranged person, and a devil. Recently, however, it is common to present three parts and one *Kyōgen*. Occasionally *Nō* and *Kyōgen* are presented especially for foreigners (an English program is provided) at the Suidōbashi Nōgakudō in Tokyo.

Nō (see ❻): **shite**, with mask, center (see ❼), jiutai, right (see ❿), **hayashi** (see ⓫)

*❼ **shite**: As a rule, the principal actor is the only one to wear the distinctive *Nō* mask, although the **shitetsure** (principal actor's assistant シテツレ) will occasionally wear a mask also. The *shite* appears as one character in the first act, and is another in the second act of the two-act drama.

*❿ **jiutai**: The *Nō* chorus and actors sing in a rather solemn style developed from Buddhist chanting.

*⓫ **hayashi**: The *Nō* ensemble consists of four instruments: a **nōkan** (*Nō* flute 能管) and three drums—a *taiko*, a *kotsuzumi*, and an **ōtsuzumi** (large hourglass-shaped drum 大鼓).

*⓬ **kagami no ma**: Literally, *kagami no ma* means "mirror room," but in English it is commonly called a "green room," meaning the room where actors wait until they are to go on stage.

*⓮ **Kyōgen**: Performed on the same stage as *Nō, Kyōgen* is a farcical form of the same art. However, *Kyōgen* is about the common people while *Nō* is about famous noblemen. As a rule, there is no music in *Kyōgen;* the actors converse rather than sing as the *Nō* performers do. *Nō* and *Kyōgen* are commonly performed together.

*⓯ **Bunraku**: *Bunraku* is also called **Ningyō Jōruri** (Puppet Theater 人形浄瑠璃). *Ningyō* means "puppet," and *jōruri* is the general term for narrative *shamisen* music, one form of which is used in *Bunraku*. The origins of *Bunraku* are in the 10th and 11th centuries, but

Bunraku (see ⓯)　　　　　　Picture courtesy of JNTO

Gidayū-bushi (see ⑲) Picture courtesy of JNTO

it did not take its present form until the 17th century when Chikamatsu Monzaemon, sometimes called Japan's greatest playwright, wrote many of his plays for *Bunraku*.

*⑯ **omozukai:** The leader of the **sanninzukai** (trio of puppeteers 三人使い) operates the puppet's head and right arm. While the others of the trio will wear masks over their entire heads, the great master will appear with no mask at all, an honor reserved for him.

*⑰ **hidarizukai:** The second of the puppeteer trio operates the left arm and hand of the puppet.

*⑱ **ashizukai:** The third man of the trio operates the legs and feet.

*⑲ **Gidayū-bushi:** *Gidayū-bushi* is the narrative *shamisen* music of *Bunraku*. This form of music was developed by Takemoto Gidayū (1651-1714) for *Bunraku*. The singer, backed up by the *shamisen*, brings life to the drama by providing the vocal expression for the puppets on stage. A single singer has such versatility that he can carry on the dialog for every character on stage.

*⑳ **Rakugo:** *Rakugo* is a type of comic story telling performed by one man. *Rakugo* is one of many acts included in **yose** (variety theater 寄席).

Rakugo (see ⑳)

❶ **sho-dō, shū-ji** (calligraphy)*
　　　　しょどう／書道，しゅうじ／習字

❷ **su-mi** (India ink, ink stick)
　　　　すみ／墨

❸ **fu-de** (brush)
　　　　ふで／筆

❹ **su-zu-ri** (inkstone)
　　　　すずり／硯

❺ **ha-n-shi** (Japanese writing paper, rice paper)*
　　　　はんし／半紙

❻ **bu-n-chi-n** (paper weight)
　　　　ぶんちん／文鎮

⑦ **mi-zu-sa-shi** (water pitcher)
　　　　みずさし／水差

❽ **su-zu-ri-ba-ko** (inkstone case)
　　　　すずりばこ／硯箱

⑨ **su-mi-e** (India ink painting, brush painting)*
　　　　すみえ／墨絵

⑩ **u-ki-yo-e** (a genre of woodblock prints)*
　　　　うきよえ／浮世絵

⑪ **ha-n-ga** (woodblock print)
　　　　はんが／版画

❷ **tō-ge-i** (ceramic art)
　　　　とうげい／陶芸

❸ **ya-ki-mo-no** (pottery, ceramic ware, china)*
　　　　やきもの／焼物

❹ **ne-n-do** (clay)
　　　　ねんど／粘土

❺ **ro-ku-ro** (potter's wheel)
　　　　ろくろ／轆轤

⑯ **ka-ma** (kiln)
　　　　かま／窯

⑰ **u-wa-gu-su-ri** (glaze)
　　　　うわぐすり／釉薬

⑱ **zō-e-n** (art of landscape gardening)*
　　　　ぞうえん／造園

⑲ **bo-n-sa-i** (miniature potted plant)*
　　　　ぼんさい／盆栽

⑳ **ne-tsu-ke** (*netsuke*)*
　　　　ねつけ／根付

NOTES:

*❶ shodō, shūji: *Shodō* literally means "the way of writing" and is the more proper name for the art of calligraphy. *Shūji* means simply "learning to write characters" but does not connote an art. In either case, of course, the subject of the writing is **kanji** (Chinese characters 漢字) and **hiragana** (the Japanese syllabary 平仮名).

*❺ hanshi: Calligraphers put characters not only on *hanshi* but also on special cards used for certain occasions: **shikishi** (large square writing card 色紙), and **tanzaku** (a long, narrow card on which odes are written 短冊).

*❾ sumie: India ink painting is a widely studied art using various shades of black India ink.

*❿ ukiyoe: Outside of Japan, *ukiyoe* are the most well known of all Japanese woodblock prints. A few of the more famous artists of *ukiyoe* are Hokusai (for his prints of Mt. Fuji), Hiroshige (for his 53 views of Tōkaidō), and Utamaro (for his beautiful women).

Ukiyoe by Hiroshige (see ❿)

*❽ yakimono: *Yakimono* literally means "baked thing" and can be used to refer to any kind of ceramic ware. However, the term *yakimono* most often refers to pottery, as opposed to **setomono** (porcelain 瀬戸物).

Karesansui
(Dry landscape,
see ⑱)

*⑱ **zōen:** Among the many beautiful gardens of Japan, two styles are especially worthy of note. One is the **shakkei** (borrowed landscape 借景) garden. This type of garden is landscaped so that it blends harmoniously with the natural trees, hills, and mountains beyond its actual borders, giving the illusion of a continuous scene of nature. The second type is the **karesansui** (dry landscape 枯山水) garden, which uses stones and rocks for its effect. For instance, gravel is often raked to give the impression of water. It is said that such gardens are especially good for contemplation.

*⑲ **bonsai:** Miniature potted plants are cultivated in such a way that they are exact miniatures of the real trees from which they were taken, complete to small leaves and flowers. Some Japanese also construct **bonkei** (tray landscapes 盆景) or **hakoniwa** (miniature gardens in a box 箱庭).

*⑳ **netsuke:** *Netsuke* are small ivory or wood carvings, originally of people or animals. They were fastened to a tobacco or other pouch and placed over the *obi* of a *kimono* to hold it in place (since the *kimono* has no pockets).

Netsuke (see ⑳)

ADDITIONAL WORDS:

tenrankai (exhibition 展覧会)
origami (art of folding paper 折紙)

In *origami*, paper is folded, without cutting or pasting, into various shapes such as a crane, a frog, a boat, or almost anything. The paper used is **irogami** (colored paper 色紙). (See also page 71.)

113

21 *Sumō:*
The National Sport of Japan

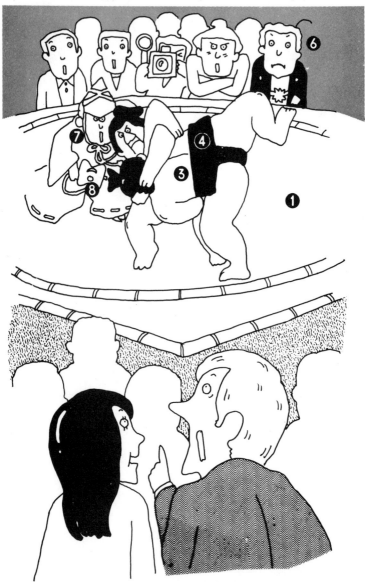

❶ **do-hyō** (ring)
   どひょう／土俵

② **do-hyō-i-ri** (entering-the-ring ceremony)*
   どひょういり／土俵入り

❸ **se-ki-to-ri** (*sumō* wrestler)*
   せきとり／関取

❹ **ma-wa-shi** (wrestler's loincloth, belt)*
   まわし／回し

⑤ **ke-shō ma-wa-shi** (ceremonial apron)*
   けしょうまわし／化粧回し

❻ **shō-bu shi-n-pa-n** (judge)*
   しょうぶしんぱん／勝負審判

❼ **gyō-ji** (referee)*
   ぎょうじ／行司

❽ **gu-n-ba-i u-chi-wa** (referee's fan)*
   ぐんばいうちわ／軍配団扇

⑨ **ba-n-zu-ke** (rankings of the wrestlers)*
   ばんづけ／番付

⑩ **ma-ku-u-chi** (upper division)*
   まくうち／幕内

⑪ **yo-ko-zu-na** (grand champion)*
   よこづな／横綱

⑫ **ō-ze-ki** (champion)*
   おおぜき／大関

⑬ **se-ki-wa-ke** (junior cHampion)
   せきわけ／関脇

⑭ **ko-mu-su-bi** (fourth rank)
   こむすび／小結

⑮ **ma-e-ga-shi-ra** (fifth rank)
   まえがしら／前頭

⑯ **jū-ryō** (junior division)
   じゅうりょう／十両

⑰ **ma-ku-shi-ta** (lower division)
   まくした／幕下

⑱ **mo-no-i-i** (judges' conference)*
   ものいい／物言

⑲ **yu-mi-to-ri-shi-ki** (bow dance)*
   ゆみとりしき／弓取式

⑳ **yū-shō** (tournament victory)
   ゆうしょう／優勝

NOTES:

Sumō: The history of *sumō*, the national sport of Japan, can be traced back as much as 1500 years, but its religious origins are still evident today in the *dohyō-iri* and other ceremonial exercises which the wrestlers perform before each bout.   However, it was only during the Edo period (1603-1868) that *sumō* took on its present form and rules, became professional, and developed into the national sport of Japan.   Today, there are six **basho** (tournaments 場所) a year: three in Tokyo (in January, May, and September at the Kuramae Kokugikan); and one each in Osaka (March), Nagoya (July), and Fukuoka (November).   Each tournament extends over a period of fifteen days, during which each wrestler fights a different opponent on each day.

*❶ **dohyō:** The *sumō* ring, about fifteen feet in diameter, is formed from bales of straw which are mostly buried in the earth.

*❷ **dohyō-iri:** Each day, before their bouts, the wrestlers will perform the entering-the-ring ceremony. *Yokozuna*, accompanied by a **tachimochi** (sword-bearer 太刀持) and a **tsuyuharai** (attendant 露払), will perform this ceremony separately.   The various movements of the ceremony are meant to symbolize the wrestler's intent to fight fairly without any weapons, and the driving of evil from the ring.

Dohyō-iri of **Yokozuna** Wajima (see ❷)

Dohyō-iri of makuuchi wrestlers (see ❷)

*❸ **sekitori:** *Sumō* wrestlers lead a hard life. Most begin training in their early teens, and they lead a stoic life in an attempt to gain admittance to the upper ranks. Wrestlers will eat and drink in large quantities in order to reach extraordinary weights of 120 kgs. (265 lbs.) or more. Technically, the term *sekitori* is reserved for the top wrestlers; a more general term is **sumōtori** (*sumō* wrestler 相撲取).

*❹ **mawashi:** About ten yards long and two feet wide, the *mawashi* is folded and wrapped around the wrestler's loins several times, depending on his size.

*❺ **keshō mawashi:** Ceremonial aprons, worn during the *dohyō-iri*, are made of silk and beautifully decorated with individual designs for each wrestler.

*❻ **shōbu shinpan:** Five judges, all retired wrestlers themselves, are seated around the *dohyō* during all upper division bouts. One of them serves as a timekeeper, and all of them watch carefully to make sure that bouts are fought fairly and that the decisions are awarded properly.

*❼ **gyōji:** The referees in *sumō* are ranked like the wrestlers, so that only a top ranking *gyōji* may officiate during a bout in which a grand champion is fighting. The referee indicates the winner of a bout by pointing his fan in the direction of the victor's side.

*❽ **gunbai uchiwa:** The rank of a *gyōji* is indicated by the color of the tassel attached to his fan: purple or purple and white for the top *gyōji*; red for *sanyaku gyōji*; red and white for *maegashira*, blue and white for *jūryō*, and blue or black for ranks below that.

*❾ banzuke: Just before each tournament, the *Sumō* Association announces the new rankings. Rankings are always adjusted for each tournament according to the records of the wrestlers in the previous tournament. Normally, **kachikoshi** (a winning record 勝越), which means the wrestler won at least eight of his fifteen bouts, assures advancement; **makekoshi** (a losing record 負越), a loss of eight or more bouts, promises a demotion in the rankings.

*❿ makuuchi: For a wrestler to enter the *makuuchi* is a great achievement. To maintain a ranking in this division is even more difficult.

*⓫ yokozuna: The grand champion is the only *sumō* wrestler assured that he will never be demoted. He will be forced to retire if he becomes too weak to maintain the winning record and the prestige required of this ranking. Over the last 300 years of *sumō*, there have been only 48 wrestlers able to achieve the coveted rank of *yokozuna*, a rank which instantly makes the holder some sort of national hero.

*⓬ ōzeki: The champion is the only wrestler who may hold his ranking even though he has a losing record in a tournament. However, if he fails to achieve a winning record in two consecutive tournaments, he will be demoted.

*⓭ monoii: When there is any doubt about who won a particular bout, one or more judges will raise their

Monoii (see ⓭)

hands to call a conference.   All five judges will then meet in the center of the ring with the referee to determine if the referee's decision (which is mandatory, whether he is sure of the victor or not) should be upheld or reversed, or if a **torinaoshi** (rematch 取直し) should be called.

*❿   **yumitorishiki:** At the end of each day's bouts, a bow dance is usually performed by a *makushita* wrestler to symbolize the gratitude of the victorious wrestlers for that day.

Yumitorishiki (see ❿)

ADDITIONAL WORDS:

sanyaku (the top three ranks below grand champion 三役)
kyō no torikumi (today's schedule of bouts きょうの取組)
kachi (win, victory 勝)

A wrestler wins his bout by forcing his opponent to touch the dirt in the ring (with some part of his body besides his feet), or to step or fall out of the ring.

make (loss, defeat 負)
[ju]-sshō, [go]-hai ([10] victories, [5] defeats [十] 勝 [五] 敗)
kantōshō (fighting spirit award 敢闘賞)
ginōshō (technique award 技能賞)
shukunshō (outstanding award 殊勲賞)
masuseki (box seat ます席)

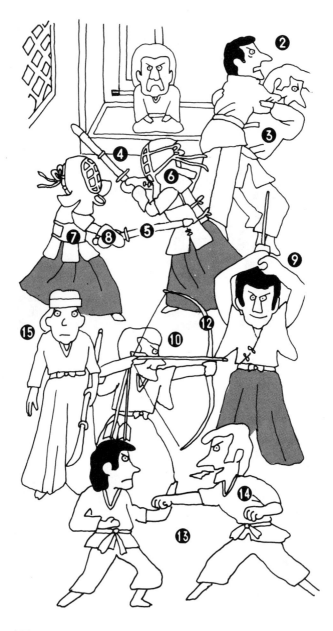

① **bu-dō** (martial arts, military science)
ぶどう／武道

❷ **jū-dō** (art of weaponless self-defense)*
じゅうどう／柔道

❸ **jū-dō-gi** (*jūdō* uniform)
じゅうどうぎ／柔道着

❹ **ke-n-dō** (Japanese art of fencing)*
けんどう／剣道

❺ **shi-na-i** (bamboo sword)
しない／竹刀

❻ **me-n** (face mask)
めん／面

❼ **dō** (chest protector)
どう／胴

❽ **ko-te** (arm guards)
こて／籠手

❾ **i-a-i-dō** (art of drawing a sword)*
いあいどう／居合道

❿ **kyū-dō** (Japanese art of archery)*
きゅうどう／弓道

⑪ **ya-bu-sa-me** (horseback archery)*
やぶさめ／流鏑馬

⑫ **yu-mi** (bow)
ゆみ／弓

⓭ **ka-ra-te** (art of weaponless self-defense)*
からて／空手

⓮ **ka-ra-te-gi** (*karate* uniform)
からてぎ／空手着

⓯ **na-gi-na-ta-dō** (art of halberd wielding)*
なぎなたどう／長刀道

⑯ **ku-sa-ri-ga-ma** (sickle and chain)*
くさりがま／鎖り鎌

⑰ **a-i-ki-dō** (another art of weaponless self-de-
あいきどう／合気道   ⌊fense)*

⑱ **dō-jō** (hall for practicing martial arts)
どうじょう／道場

⑲ **bu-shi-dō** (the way of the *samurai*)*
ぶしどう／武士道

⑳ **sa-mu-ra-i, bu-shi** (Japanese warrior)*
さむらい／侍，ぶし／武士

NOTES:

*❷ **jūdō:** *Jūdō* is perhaps the most popular of Japan's traditional martial arts. It was developed about a century ago from **jūjutsu** (a form of weaponless self-defense 柔術) by one Professor Kano who founded the Kōdōkan, an institute for *jūdō*. He refined several kinds of *jūjutsu* into the martial art that he called *jūdō*, the forerunner of modern *jūdō*.

Jū literally means "gentleness," and the combination *jūdō* literally means "the way of gentleness." Basically, this martial art involves training the body and mind so that the practitioner may defend himself victoriously without resisting his opponent. That is, the individual will give into the strength and power of his opponent in such a way that he may turn aside his opponent's attack and even turn it to his own advantage. The techniques used in *jūdō* can be divided into three groups learned in this order: **nagewaza** (the art of throwing 投げ技), **katamewaza** (the art of grappling 固め技), and finally **atemi** (the art of attacking the vital points of the body 当て身).

Today, these techniques have been adapted to make *jūdō* a competitive sport. It has gained such popularity that *jūdō* has been one of the events of the international Olympics since 1964.

Judo (see ❷) as practiced by women

122

Kendō (see ❹)

*❹ **kendō**: Japanese fencing developed into a refined martial art of the *samurai* during the Muromachi Period (1392-1573). However, it was during the Edo Period (1603-1868) that protective apparel and the bamboo sword were introduced, making it possible to have *kendō* contests without the danger of someone being injured seriously. *Kendō* has not become an international sport, but it is practiced earnestly by thousands of Japanese.

*❾ **iaidō**: *Iaidō* is closely related to *kendō*, the most obvious difference being the use of real swords. Since opponents must be imaginary, form in drawing, wielding and sheathing the **katana** (sword 刀) is emphasized.

Katana (see note ❾) on display

*❿ **kyūdō**: In *kyūdō*, the archer concentrates as much on having the proper attitude and form as on hitting the target.

123

Yabusame (see ⑪) Picture courtesy of JNTO

*⑪ **yabusame:** An exhibition of this ancient practice is given every year in Kamakura on the 16th of September during the Tsurugaoka Hachimangū Shrine Festival. Archers, dressed in traditional costumes, ride their horses past a wooden target while shooting arrows at it, a colorful reminder of days gone by.

*⑬ **karate:** *Karate* was developed in Okinawa (after being introduced from China) as a method of self-defense when the Tokugawa Shogunate took all the weapons away from the Okinawan people. *Karate* became especially popular in Japan after World War II when the occupation forces banned all other martial arts.

Karate literally means "empty hand," and is a rather spectacular martial art. With their bare hands, practitioners break bricks and piles of wood in seemingly effortless blows. It is said that the *karate* expert can even inflict a mortal wound to either man or beast with a single blow of the fist.

124

*⓯ **naginatadō**: The halberd was once used in actual combat in the 12th, 13th, and 14th centuries, but was later replaced by the spear. Now, halberd wielding is practiced only by women, who will use wooden and bamboo halberds in contest matches.

*⓰ **kusarigama**: In actual combat, the chain of the *kusarigama* was used to disarm and weaken the enemy, and the sickle was used to complete the attack. In contests today, a wooden sickle and rope are used as substitutes for the actual sickle and chain.

*⓱ **aikidō**: Like *jūdō*, *aikidō* is a method of weaponless self-defense developed from *jūjutsu*. However, it differs in some respects, most noticeably in the clothing worn, but also in techniques. Practitioners of *aikidō* emphasize the importance of **ki** (mind, spirit 気) which must be strong in order to defend themselves successfully, since technique itself is not enough.

*⓳ **bushidō**: *Bushidō* (sometimes compared to the chivalry of the knights in Europe during the middle ages) refers to an unwritten code of ethics which governed the lives and behavior of the *samurai*, or warrior class, during the middle ages of Japan.

*⓴ **samurai, bushi**: The Japanese *samurai* were the retainers of the **daimyō** (feudal lords 大名), the leaders of the Japanese clans. Loyalty was the most important virtue for these warriors, for they thought nothing of giving their lives for their overlords.

Aikidō (see ⓱)

125

23 Shrines and *Shintō*

❶ **ji-n-ja** (shrine)*
じんじゃ／神社

❷ **to-ri-i** (shrine entrance)*
とりい／鳥居

③ **sa-n-dō** (approach to a shrine)
さんどう／参道

④ **ta-ma-ga-ki** (fence of a shrine)
たまがき／玉垣

❺ **te-mi-zu-ya** (ablution pavilion)*
てみずや／手水舎

❻ **shi-n-de-n** (sanctuary)
しんでん／神殿

❼ **sha-mu-sho** (shrine office)
しゃむしょ／社務所

⑧ **shi-me-na-wa** (sacred straw rope with short
しめなわ／注連縄　　⌊paper streamers)*

❾ **sa-i-se-n-ba-ko** (offering box)*
さいせんばこ／賽銭箱

⑩ **(o-)sa-i-se-n** (offertory, offering of money)
（お）さいせん／（お）賽銭

⑪ **(o-)mi-ku-ji** (fortune, written oracle)*
（お）みくじ／（お）神籤

⑫ **(o-)mi-ki** (sacred wine)*
（お）みき／（お）神酒

❸ **ka-n-nu-shi(-sa-n)** (*Shintō* priest)
かんぬし（さん）／神主（さん）

⑭ **sha-ku** (mace, symbol of the office of priest)
しゃく／笏

❺ **mi-ko** (priestess)
みこ／巫子

⑯ **Shi-n-tō** (*Shintō*, the way of the gods)*
しんとう／神道

⑰ **ka-mi** (gods, God, deity)
かみ／神

⑱ **no-ri-to** (*Shintō* prayer)
のりと／祝詞

⑲ **mi-ko-shi** (sacred palanquin, portable shrine)*
みこし／神輿

⑳ **shi-n-ze-n ke-kko-n-shi-ki** (*Shintō* wedding)*
しんぜんけっこんしき／神前結婚式

NOTES:

*❶ **jinja:** The *Shintō* shrine is a place of worship and the place in which the *Shintō* gods are believed to reside. There are tens of thousands of shrines, large and small, located all over Japan.

*❷ **torii:** This structure, found at the entrance to most shrines, symbolically separates the holy world inside from the secular world outside.

*❺ **temizuya:** At the ablution pavilion, visitors will rinse their mouths and pour water over their hands as an act of purification to prepare them for worship.

*❽ **shimenawa:** The *shimenawa* is usually hung between pillars to indicate the entrance to a sacred place, especially where gods are supposed to dwell.

Shimenawa (see ❽)

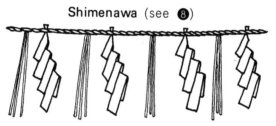

*❾ **saisenbako:** A visitor will drop an offering, usually in coins, into the *saisenbako* or offering box found in front of the sanctuary whenever he goes to pray at a shrine.

*⓫ **(o)mikuji:** Written oracles are usually sold (along with postcards of the shrine and other items) at a small stand near the main sanctuary.   From a box, the visitor will draw a stick with a number on it indicating what oracle he is to receive.   After reading his fortune, the visitor will fold it and wrap it around a tree branch to bring good luck.

*⓬ **(o)miki:** Sacred wine (actually *sake*) is that which is offered to the gods.

*⓰ **Shintō:** The word *Shintō* comes from two characters: *shin*, which is also read as *kami* and means "god" or "gods"; and *tō* which means "way." Therefore, *Shintō* is the "way of the gods." *Shintō* is the indigenous

Mikoshi (see ⑲) Picture courtesy of JNTO

religion of the Japanese people. There is no single great figure in *Shintō* (like Christ or Buddha) from whom the faith developed and received a body of teaching. Rather, *Shintō* is a collection of beliefs and ideas about the proper way of behavior which has developed over two thousand years.

*⑲ **mikoshi:** During festivals, portable shrines are carried through the streets by men and boys wearing *happi* coats and shouting "*wasshoi, wasshoi,*" a phrase with no meaning except to encourage themselves in carrying the heavy *mikoshi*. It is believed that the spirit of the *kami* is transferred from the shrine's sanctuary to the portable shrine for this ride through the streets.

*⑳ **shinzen kekkonshiki:** The *Shintō* wedding ceremony is traditional more than it is religious. In Japan, most weddings are performed according to the rites of *Shintō*, while funerals are conducted according to Buddhist rites. This is an apparent contradiction to many foreigners, but not to the Japanese who feel no compulsion to give one hundred percent allegiance to either religion.

① **(o-)te-ra** (temple)*
   （お）てら／（お）寺

② **sa-n-mo-n** (temple gate)*
   さんもん／山門

③ **ho-n-dō** (main building of the temple)
   ほんどう／本堂

④ **ka-ne-tsu-ki-dō** (bell tower)
   かねつきどう／鐘撞堂

⑤ **tsu-ri-ga-ne** (temple bell)*
   つりがね／釣鐘

⑥ **tō** (pagoda, tower)
   とう／塔

❼ **(o-)bō-sa-n, sō-ryo** (priest, monk)
   （お）ぼうさん／（お）坊さん，そうりょ／僧侶

❽ **ke-sa** (surplice)
   けさ／袈裟

❾ **ju-zu** (rosary)
   じゅず／珠数

❿ **ga-sshō** (gesture of raising the hands, palm to
   がっしょう／合掌   ⌊palm)*

⓫ **(o-)kyō** (sutras, Buddhist scriptures)*
   （お）きょう／（お）経

⑫ **mo-ku-gyo** (slit gong used in Buddhist chanting)
   もくぎょう／木魚

⑬ **Bu-kkyō** (Buddhism)*
   ぶっきょう／仏教

⑭ **Sha-ka** (Sakya, Buddha)
   しゃか／釈迦

⓯ **bu-tsu-zō** (image of Buddha)
   ぶつぞう／仏像

⑯ **za-ze-n** (silent meditation, religious meditation)*
   ざぜん／座禅

⑰ **e-n-ni-chi** (temple or shrine fair)*
   えんにち／縁日

⑱ **sō-shi-ki** (funeral)*
   そうしき／葬式

⑲ **ha-ka** (grave, tomb)*
   はか／墓

⓴ **se-n-kō** (incense stick)*
   せんこう／線香

NOTES:

*❶ (o)tera: Temples are found throughout Japan, an indication of the large influence which Buddhism has had upon the Japanese culture. The size of the temples varies from a small single structure to large compounds including a main hall, a lecture hall, living quarters, and other structures as well. The name for particular temples often ends with the character for *tera*, which may also be read *-ji*, as in Ryōanji and Enkakuji, two famous temples in Japan.

*❷ sanmon: The *sanmon* marks the entrance to a temple just as the *torii* marks the entrance to a shrine.

*❺ tsurigane: The temple bell is also called **ōgane** (big bell 大鐘). Besides its normal use, it is rung 108 times at New Years to exorcise the 108 sins of the last year and to welcome the fresh new year.

*❿ gasshō: This gesture is performed to show respect, thankfulness, and/or humility.

*⓫ (o)kyō: The sutras are the scriptures of Buddhism. It is believed that they are the teachings and sayings of Shakyamuni Buddha.

*⓭ Bukkyō: There are two main divisions of Buddhism: a southern branch called **Shōjō** (Small Vehicle 小乗) and a northern branch called **Daijō** (Great Vehicle 大乗). The latter of these is the one which found its way to Japan in about the sixth century. In Japan now, there are several sects which emphasize different sutra, the main four being the Tendai sect, the Jōdō sect, the

Sanmon (see ❷)   Tsurigane (see ❺)

Ennichi (see ⓱) at Tōji in Kyoto

Zen sect, and the Shingon sect. *Bukkyō* is, of course, one of the two main religions in Japan (the other being *Shintō*).

*⓰ **zazen**: The Zen sect of Buddhism practices silent meditation as a way to attain **satori** (enlightenment 悟り). It is said that *zazen* (and *satori*) cannot be explained adequately in words; they must be experienced to be understood.

*⓱ **ennichi**: Temple festival days are special occasions when the gods or Buddha and all men are supposed to be unified. As a part of the celebration on these days, merchants will set up stalls selling items of every description from clothes to musical instruments. In Kyoto, two big *ennichi* afford an excellent opportunity to buy antiques at bargain prices. These festivals are held on the 21st of each month at Tōji and on the 25th of each month at Kitano Tenmangū.

*⓲ **sōshiki**: Japanese funerals are generally performed according to Buddhist tradition (although weddings are usually *Shintō*).

*⓳ **haka**: The *haka* is located in a **bochi** (graveyard 墓地), and is visited by the survivors of the immediate family.

*⓴ **senkō**: Incense is burned at most Buddhist ceremonies and at the graveyard. It is also found at the entrance to some temples so that the visitor may wave the smoke onto his head in a symbolic act of purification, which is believed to improve his mind.

25 Japanese Holidays and Festivals

春 ⑯ ⑰

夏 ⑬ ⑭

秋 ⑳

冬

❶

134

❶ Shō-ga-tsu (New Year's Days)*
しょうがつ／正月

② Se-i-ji-n no hi (Adult's Day)*
せいじんのひ／成人の日

③ Ke-n-ko-ku ki-ne-n-bi (National Foundation
けんこくきねんび／建国記念日　　　⌊Day)*

④ Shu-n-bu-n no hi (Vernal Equinox Day)*
しゅんぶんのひ／春分の日

⑤ Te-n-nō ta-n-jō-bi (Emperor's Birthday)*
てんのうたんじょうび／天皇誕生日

⑥ Ke-n-pō ki-ne-n-bi (Constitution Memorial
けんぽうきねんび／憲法記念日　　　⌊Day)*

⑦ Ko-do-mo no hi (Children's Day)*
こどものひ／子供の日

⑧ Ke-i-rō no hi (Respect-for-the-Aged Day)*
けいろうのひ／敬老の日

⑨ Shū-bu-n no hi (Autumnal Equinox Day)*
しゅうぶんのひ／秋分の日

⑩ Ta-i-i-ku no hi (Sports Day)*
たいいくのひ／体育の日

⑪ Bu-n-ka no hi (Culture Day)*
ぶんかのひ／文化の日

⑫ Ki-n-rō-ka-n-sha no hi (Labor Thanksgiving
きんろうかんしゃのひ／勤労感謝の日　⌊Day)*

❸ ma-tsu-ri (festival)
まつり／祭

❹ mi-ko-shi (sacred palanquin, a portable shrine)
みこし／神輿

⑮ Hi-na-ma-tsu-ri (Doll's Festival, Girl's Festival)*
ひなまつり／雛祭り

❻ Ta-n-go no se-kku (Boy's Festival)*
たんごのせっく／端午の節句

❼ ko-i-no-bo-ri (carp streamer)*
こいのぼり／鯉幟

⑱ (o-)bo-n (*Bon* Festival, Buddhist All Souls'
（お）ぼん／（お）盆　　　　　　　⌊Day)*

⑲ Ta-na-ba-ta (Festival of the Weaver)*
たなばた／七夕

❿ Shi-chi-go-san (A Day for Children of three, five
しちごさん／七五三　　　　　⌊and seven)*

135

NOTES:

*❶ Shōgatsu: Although the term *Shōgatsu* (polite: *Oshōgatsu*) literally means the "first month," New Year's Days run from the first of January to the third. The first of January itself is called **Ganjitsu** (New Year's Day 元日), and is the first of twelve national holidays in Japan. *Oshōgatsu* is undoubtedly the most important of all the Japanese holidays.

Before the end of the year, the Japanese send **nengajō** (New Year's cards 年賀状) to their friends and acquaintances, a custom similar to that of sending Christmas cards. These cards are not delivered immediately; the post office holds them until the first of January when they are delivered all at once.

Other traditions are the **hatsumōde** (first visit (to a shrine or temple) 初詣) and the first performance of some special art, such as **kakizome** (the first writing of calligraphy 書初) or **hatsugama** (the first tea ceremony 初釜). Japanese also eat special foods during *Oshōgatsu*, including **(o)mochi** (rice cakes (お)餅), which is sometimes prepared in a special soup and called **(o)zōni** (rice cakes boiled with vegetables (お)雑煮). There is also the traditional first drink of **(o)toso** (special spiced *sake* for New Year's (お)屠蘇).

It is customary to say **akemashite omedetō gozaimasu** (Happy New Year 明けましておめでとうございます) the first time you see your friends or acquaintances in the new year.

Hatsumode (see ❶) at Meiji Jingu Shrine in Tokyo

Koinobori (see ⑰)   Picture courtesy of JNTO

*❷ **Seijin no hi:** January 15. The 2nd national holiday. This day is set aside to honor 20 year olds, who legally become adults at that age.

*❸ **Kenkoku kinenbi:** February 11. The 3rd national holiday.

*❹ **Shunbun no hi:** About February 21. The 4th national holiday.

*❺ **Tennō tanjōbi:** April 29. The 5th national holiday. This is the first holiday of **gōruden uiiku** (golden week ゴールデンウィーク), so called because it contains three holidays very close together.

*❻ **Kenpō kinenbi:** May 3. The 6th national holiday. Constitution Memorial Day celebrates the establishment of the modern Japanese Constitution on May 3, 1947.

*❼ **Kodomo no hi:** May 5. The 7th national holiday.

*❽ **Keirō no hi:** September 15. The 8th national holiday.

*❾ **Shūbun no hi:** About September 23. The 9th national holiday.

*❿ **Taiiku no hi:** October 10. The 10th national holiday.

*⓫ **Bunka no hi:** November 3. The 11th national holiday. Among the many activities held to encourage the arts, **bunkasai** (cultural festivals 文化祭) are held at schools and universities throughout Japan on or around Culture Day.

*⓬ **Kinrōkansha no hi:** November 23. The 12th and last national holiday.

*⓮ **mikoshi:** See also "Shrines and *Shintō*," p. 129.

Picture courtesy of JNTO

A display of hinaningyō for Hinamatsuri (see ⓯)

*⓯ **Hinamatsuri:** March 3. The Doll's Festival is a special celebration for girls, whose homes usually have a display of hinaningyō (*hina* dolls 雛人形) to mark the occasion.

*⓰ **Tango no sekku:** May 5. Now this day coincides with Children's Day, the national holiday, but it is still special for boys.

*⓱ **koinobori:** Carp streamers are symbolic of the strength and perserverence that boys need, just as the carp needs these qualities to swim upstream. *Koinobori* are displayed outside of homes with boys on May 5, Boy's Festival.

*⓲ **(O)bon:** *Bon* Festival is a summer event held in honor of those who have passed away. It is believed that the spirits of the dead return for a brief period, and

Bon'odori (see ⓲)　　　　　　Picture courtesy of JNTO

the Japanese comfort them in various ways while they are here, before sending them away again. Everyone participates in community folk dances called **Bon'odori** (*Bon* dances 盆踊り), which is easily recognizable by the **ōdaiko** (big drum 大太鼓) that sits in the middle of a circle of dancers and is played with a deep boom.

*⑲ **Tanabata**: July 7. *Tanabata*, according to legend, is the day that two stars—**Orihime** (Vega, the Weaver 織姫) and her lover **Kengyū** (Altair 牽牛)—meet in the skies over Japan. The seventh day of the seventh month is the only day they are permitted to see each other since they once allowed their affection for each other to interfere with their heavenly tasks. So this happy day is enough of an excuse for the Japanese to have a festival. *Tanabata* is especially appreciated in Sendai and Hiratsuka where their festivals have become famous.

*⑳ **Shichigosan**: November 15. *Shichigosan* literally means "seven-five-three." On this day, girls of three and seven and boys of five are dressed up in their finest clothes, Western or Japanese, and taken to the shrines. Here, everyone prays for their continued growth and good health.

Tsukimi (Moon viewing)

ADDITIONAL WORDS:

hanami (cherry blossom viewing 花見)

Every year, around the first of April, depending on the weather conditions, the **sakura no hana** (cherry blossoms 桜の花) come out, signifying the arrival of spring. At this time it is traditional to go wherever the cherry blossoms may be viewed. Japanese also enjoy viewing **yozakura** (cherry blossoms at night 夜桜).

tsukimi (moon viewing 月見)

Japanese enjoy looking at the moon in mid-autumn when it is supposed to be the most beautiful.

26 Japanese Bath

❶ **(o-)fu-ro** (bath)*
    （お）ふろ／（お）風呂

② **se-n-tō** (public bath)*
    せんとう／銭湯

③ **o-n-se-n** (hot spring)*
    おんせん／温泉

④ **tō-ji** (hot spring cure)*
    とうじ／湯治

⑤ **no-te-n-bu-ro** (open air bath)*
    のてんぶろ／野天風呂

⑥ **ko-n-yo-ku** (mixed bathing)*
    こんよく／混浴

⑦ **o-to-ko-yu** (men's section of the bath)
    おとこゆ／男湯

⑧ **o-n-na-yu** (women's section of the bath)
    おんなゆ／女湯

⑨ **ba-n-da-i** (fee collector's stand)
    ばんだい／番台

⑩ **fu-ro-da-i** (bathing fee)*
    ふろだい／風呂代

⑪ **fu-ro-ba** (bathroom)
    ふろば／風呂場

❷ **sa-n-su-ke(-sa-n)** (bathhouse attendant)*
    さんすけ（さん）／三助（さん）

❸ **(o-)yu** (hot water)
    （お）ゆ／（お）湯

❹ **mi-zu** (cold water)
    みず／水

❺ **se-kke-n** (soap)
    せっけん／石鹸

❻ **o-ke** (bucket, pail)*
    おけ／桶

⑰ **se-n-me-n-ki** (washbowl, washbasin)*
    せんめんき／洗面器

❽ **te-nu-gu-i** (Japanese towel)*
    てぬぐい／手拭

⑲ **ta-o-ru** (towel)*
    タオル

❿ **he-chi-ma** (sponge gourd)*
    へちま／糸瓜

NOTES:

*❶ (o)furo: The Japanese bath is not simply for washing. The Japanese take a bath to relax, to forget their problems, and to renew themselves for the tasks of their daily lives. All washing is done outside the tub, which is kept full of clean water and may be used several times before being changed. After washing and rinsing thoroughly, the bather will ease himself into the steaming hot water and soak for a few minutes before reluctantly climbing out and returning to the hectic world.

*❷ sentō: Public baths are slowly beginning to disappear, but many Japanese still use them since their homes do not have private baths. The best time to go to the *sentō* is just after it opens at about three o'clock, because the water is the freshest then.

*❸ onsen: Natural hot springs have become rather popular resorts in Japan. People go there not only for the baths, but also to escape the city and to relax.

*❹ tōji: Another reason that many people go to the *onsen* is because of the mineral content in the water which is believed to be good for their ailments.

*❺ notenburo: Japanese like the outdoor bath because it is possible to enjoy nature at the same time that they bathe.

Notenburo (see ❺)　　　　　Picture courtesy of JNTO

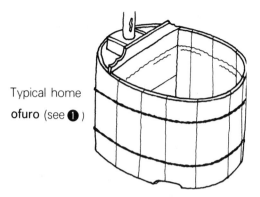

Typical home
ofuro (see **❶**)

***❻** kon'yoku: Mixed bathing is not so common a practice as it once was, but there are still a few baths where it is allowed.

***❿** furodai: The bathing fee for *sentō* in Tokyo is currently about 240 yen.

***⓬** sansuke: A bathhouse attendant is still found in a few *sentō*, but he has largely disappeared. His duties included scrubbing and massaging the bather's back.

***⓰** oke: The *oke* is made out of wood and is provided by the bathhouse for the bather's use while he is there.

***⓱** senmenki: The *senmenki* is a small washbasin made out of plastic or metal (not wood). Japanese who regularly go to the public bath often find it convenient to provide their own washbasin rather than use an *oke* provided at the *sentō* since these latter are limited in number.

***⓲** tenugui: This towel is made of a simply woven, cotton material about two and a half feet long and a foot wide. The same *tenugui* is used for both washing and drying.

***⓳** taoru: This is the Western-style, terry-cloth towel which comes in many different sizes. It may be used in the same way as the *tenugui*, or it may be used merely for drying oneself.

***⓴** hechima: A sponge gourd is a plant that was found to be useful in taking a bath. It is something like a stiff sponge and is very good for scrubbing.

27Japanese Apparel

① **ki-mo-no** (Japanese robe, clothes)*
きもの／着物

❷ **yu-ka-ta** (light cotton *kimono*)*
ゆかた／浴衣

❸ **ta-n-ze-n** (thick *kimono*)*
たんぜん／丹前

❹ **ha-o-ri** (Japanese coat)*
はおり／羽織

❺ **ha-ka-ma** (divided skirt for men's formal wear)*
はかま／袴

❻ **o-bi** (belt, sash)
おび／帯

❼ **o-bi-do-me** (*obi* tie, sash clip)
おびどめ／帯止

⑧ **o-bi-a-ge** (sash bustle)
めおびあげ／帯上

⑨ **ko-shi-hi-mo** (waist tie)
げこじひも／腰紐

❿ **ha-o-ri no hi-mo** (*haori* tie)
はおりのひも／羽織の紐

⑪ **na-ga-ju-ba-n** (long undergarment)
ながじゅばん／長襦袢

⑫ **ta-bi** (Japanese socks)
たび／足袋

❸ **ge-ta** (clogs)
げた／下駄

❹ **zō-ri** (sandals)
ぞうり／草履

⑮ **a-shi-da** (high *geta* for rainy weather)
あしだ／足駄

❻ **mo-n, mo-n-shō** (family crest, coat of arms)*
もん／紋，もんしょう／紋章

⑰ **mo-n-tsu-ki** (*kimono* with crest)
もんつき／紋付

❽ **fu-ri-so-de** (long-sleeved *kimono*)*
ふりそで／振袖

⑲ **so-ku-ta-i** (ancient ceremonial court dress for
そくたい／束帯 ⌊men)

⑳ **jū-ni-hi-to-e** (ancient ceremonial court dress for
じゅうにひとえ／十二単衣 ⌊women)

145

NOTES:

*❶ **kimono:** The modern *kimono* has remained largely unchanged since the beginning of this century. However, habits of wearing the *kimono* are changing noticeably. Although older people continue to wear *kimono* often, younger people tend to wear *kimono* only on very special occasions such as New Year's or weddings. This trend can be explained in terms of practicality: the *kimono* does not allow much freedom of movement and is not the most comfortable of garments, even if it is one of the most beautiful.

Kimono, *yukata* and *tanzen* may be purchased at stores specializing in Japanese clothing, called *gofukuya*, or in department stores. Although ready-made *kimono* are available, it is more common to have them made to order.

*❷ **yukata:** The *yukata* is an informal garment worn in summer since it is much cooler than *kimono*. (See also the note on page 36.)

*❸ **tanzen:** The *tanzen* is thick and warm, so it is worn informally during cold weather. *Ryokan* often provide them for their guests during the winter.

*❹ **haori:** The *haori* is worn over the *kimono* in cold weather.

*❺ **hakama:** Worn only on very formal occasions, the *hakama* is a kind of loose-legged trousers for men, but is sometimes worn by women too.

Happi (*Happi* coat)

Pictures from *Shōzoku-Zufu* by permission

Sokutai (see ⑲)   Jūnihitoe (see ⑳)

*⑯   **mon, monshō:** Each Japanese family has its own crest which is put on their formal kimono.

*⑱   **furisode:** The long-sleeve *kimono* is traditionally worn only by single girls on formal occasions.

ADDITIONAL WORDS:

happi (*happi* coat, workman's garment はっぴ)

   Worn originally by firemen and certain servants in the Edo Period, the *happi* coat became a workman's garment for fishmongers and carpenters. Today, visitors to Japan buy them as souvenirs and use them as a kind of dressing-gown.

haramaki (waistband, a health band 腹巻)

   The *haramaki* is worn to keep the abdomen warm in the belief that this will keep the wearer healthy. It is commonly worn even in hot weather.

mofuku (mourning dress 喪服)

katsura (wig かつら)

❶ **go** (*go*, the national board game of Japan)*
ご／碁

❷ **go-ba-n** (*go* board)
ごばん／碁盤

❸ **go-i-shi** (*go* stone)
ごいし／碁石

❹ **go-ke** (*go* stone box)
ごけ／碁笥

⑤ **go-ka-i-sho** (*go* club)
ごかいしょ／碁会所

❻ **go-mo-ku-na-ra-be** (simplified version of *go*)*
ごもくならべ／五目並べ

❼ **shō-gi** (Japanese chess)*
しょうぎ／将棋

❽ **shō-gi-ba-n** (*shōgi* board)
しょうぎばん／将棋盤

❾ **shō-gi no ko-ma** (*shōgi* men, pieces)
しょうぎのこま／将棋の駒

❿ **mā-ja-n** (mahjong)*
マージャン／麻雀

⑪ **mā-ja-n-ya** (mahjong parlor)
マージャンや／麻雀屋

⑫ **pa-i** (mahjong tile)
パイ／牌

⑬ **sa-i-ko-ro** (die, dice)
さいころ／骰子

⑭ **pa-chi-n-ko** (Japanese pinball game)*
パチンコ

⑮ **pa-chi-n-ko-ya** (*pachinko* parlor)
パチンコや／パチンコ屋

⑯ **ha-na-fu-da** (Japanese playing cards, flower cards)*
はなふだ／花札

⑰ **ka-ru-ta** (Japanese cards)*
かるた

⑱ **hya-ku-ni-n-i-sshu** (the cards of one hundred famous poems)*
ひゃくにんいっしゅ／百人一首

⑲ **ta-ko-a-ge** (kite-flying)*
たこあげ／凧揚げ

⑳ **ko-ma-ma-wa-shi** (top-spinning)*
こままわし／独楽回し

NOTES:

*❶ go: *Go* is an extremely difficult game of strategy in which the players (two) attempt to capture territory by surrounding space on the board with their stones (either white or black). The rules themselves are rather simple, and can be learned rather quickly. However, the strategy is extraordinarily complicated. *Go* has been compared to a full-scale war, whereas chess or *shōgi* is a "mere" battle. In other words, *go* players must watch several battles on the same board at all times, and the loss of a particular battle does not necessarily mean a loss of the war.

A top quality *go* board (marked with 19 vertical and 19 horizontal lines forming 361 points of intersection) and stones (181 black, 180 white) can be quite expensive, although a simple folding board and plastic stones can be purchased at reasonable prices.

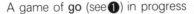

A game of **go** (see❶) in progress

*❻ gomokunarabe: Played with the same equipment as *go*, *gomokunarabe* is a much simpler game in which the object is to arrange five stones in a row. Although it is harder than it looks, anyone can play this game, whereas *go* requires a great deal of study to gain even a modicum of skill.

Pachinko-ya (see ⓮ and ⓯)

*❼ **shōgi:** *Shōgi* is very much like chess in the West although the pieces move in somewhat different ways. The unique feature of *shōgi* is that pieces are never removed from the game entirely. When an opponent's piece is captured, it may be reintroduced into the game as a part of the captor's own forces by placing it in any vacant space on the board during any of his subsequent turns. As a result, it is impossible to have a draw as in Western chess—someone always wins.

As with *go*, *shōgi* equipment can be very expensive, but a simple folding board (9 rows of 9 spaces) and men (40 pieces altogether, 20 for each player) can be purchased at a reasonable price.

*⓾ **mājan:** Mahjong, a game of Chinese origin, is not so much a game of skill as *go* and *shōgi* are; luck is a factor in the game as well. Mahjong is played by four persons, and it allows for much more socializing.

*⓮ **pachinko:** There is a *pachinko* parlor in front of nearly every railroad station in Tokyo, a fact which testifies to the popularity of the game. Luck plays a part

Pachinko machine (see ⓮)

151

in this game also, since some machines are said to work better than others.

*⑯ **hanafuda**: *Hana* literally means "flower" while *fuda* means "cards," so the combination means "flower cards." Sometimes called **hanagaruta** (flower cards 花がるた) *hanafuda* are gaily decorated with flowers and other designs. The game is usually played by 3 to 6 people and involves a bit of friendly betting.

*⑰ **karuta**: *Karuta* is a general term for various Japanese cards used in different games. For Western cards, the word **toranpu** (cards トランプ) is used.

Hyakunin'isshu (see ⑱)   Picture courtesy of JNTO

*⑱ **hyakunin'isshu**: In *hyakunin'isshu*, the goal is to match two cards with different parts of the same poem written on them. The person who matches the most poems (there are 100 altogether) is declared the winner. This game is commonly played during *Oshōgatsu*.

Picture courtesy of JNTO
Hanetsuki using the **hagoita** (see note ⑲)

*⑲ **takoage**: Japanese kites are gaily decorated with paintings of dragons, *ukiyoe*, or *Kabuki* actors and come in many shapes and sizes. *Takoage* is a pastime enjoyed by boys at almost any time of year, but it is especially popular at New Year's. Another popular activity for girls at New Year's time is **hanetsuki** (Japanese badminton 羽根つき), using the colorful **hagoita** (battledore 羽子板).

*⑳ **komamawashi**: There are many kinds of colorful **koma** (tops 独楽) in Japan, and at New Year's, *komamawashi* is a popular activity for boys.

USEFUL EXPRESSIONS:

1. **Go wa dekimasu ka?**
   (Can you play *go*?)
   碁はできますか.
2. **Shōgi o oshiete kuremasen ka?**
   (Will you teach me to play *shogi*?)
   将棋を教えてくれませんか.
3. **dan** (grade, rank) 段
   Go wa nan-dan desu ka?
   (What rank are you in *go*?)
   碁は何段ですか.
   [Ni]-dan desu.
   (I am [second] rank.)
   [二] 段です.

Tako (kite, see ⑲)

153

❶　**ge-n-ka-n** (entrance hall)*
　　げんかん／玄関

❷　**ge-ta-ba-ko** (clog (and shoe) cabinet)
　　げたばこ／下駄箱

❸　**rō-ka** (corridor, hallway)
　　ろうか／廊下

④　**wa-shi-tsu** (Japanese-style room)
　　わしつ／和室

⑤　**ta-ta-mi** (*tatami* mat)*
　　たたみ／畳

❻　**to-ko-no-ma** (alcove)*
　　とこのま／床の間

❼　**ka-ke-ji-ku** (hanging scroll)*
　　かけじく／掛け軸

❽　**ta-n-su** (chest of drawers)
　　たんす／簞笥

⑨　**o-shi-i-re** (closet)
　　おしいれ／押入れ

❿　**shō-ji** (sliding screen papered on one side)*
　　しょうじ／障子

⓫　**fu-su-ma** (sliding partition)*
　　ふすま／襖

⑫　**a-ma-do** (storm door, shutter)
　　あまど／雨戸

⑬　**kya-ku-ma** (guest room)
　　きゃくま／客間

⓮　**i-ma** (living room)
　　いま／居間

⑮　**da-i-do-ko-ro** (kitchen)
　　だいどころ／台所

⑯　**hi-ba-chi** (brazier)
　　ひばち／火鉢

⓱　**ko-ta-tsu** (foot warmer)*
　　こたつ／火燵

⑱　**ka-mi-da-na** (household alter)*
　　かみだな／神棚

⓳　**bu-tsu-da-n** (household Buddhist shrine)*
　　ぶつだん／仏壇

⑳　**ni-wa** (garden)
　　にわ／庭

NOTES:

*❶ **genkan:** When entering a Japanese house, you should always leave your shoes in the entrance hall; shoes are never worn inside.

*❺ **tatami:** *Tatami* mats are the typical flooring material in a Japanese home. Although slippers may be worn in parts of a Japanese house where the floor is wooden, they should not be worn into a *tatami* room. (See also the note on page 36.)

*❻ **tokonoma:** The *tokonoma* is traditionally found in the best room of the Japanese house. When the family entertains, the guest of honor will be asked to sit in front of the *tokonoma*.

*❼ **kakejiku:** Traditionally hung in the *tokonoma*, the *kakejiku* is a scroll on which a picture has been painted or characters have been written.

*❿ **shōji:** *Shōji* are made of a wooden frame covered on one side by white paper. Light will be diffused through the paper, which cannot be seen through, so *shōji* are used as a kind of curtain.

*⓫ **fusuma:** *Fusuma* are also made of a wooden frame, but they are covered on both sides by paper on which a picture or design is sometimes printed. No light will pass through the *fusuma*, so they are used as partitions between rooms or as doors to closets.

Shōji being re-papered (see ❿)

*⓱ **kotatsu:** During the winter, a *kotatsu* is often used to keep the legs and feet warm. Traditionally, charcoal was put under the *kotatsu,* but today special electric heating units are commonly used.

*⓲ **kamidana:** The *kamidana* is a shelf for the *kami* of *Shintō.* On the shelf, the Japanese family will put a miniature shrine and other articles of faith. An **(o)fuda** (talisman (お)札) of **Ise Jingū** (Grand Shrine of Ise 伊勢神宮) is usually placed inside the shrine along with one for the **ujigami** (tutelary diety 氏神). Fresh offerings of rice, water, and salt (or other foods on special occasions) are also placed on the shelf.

*⓳ **butsudan:** The *butsudan* usually holds a figure of the Buddha and a tablet with the names of the family dead. Flowers and food are offered, incense is burned, and sutras are chanted at the *butsudan.* It is not uncommon for one family to have both a *butsudan* and a *kamidana.*

Kamidana (see ⓲)

DIALOG:

(Arriving at the Tanaka residence)

Jones: Gomen kudasai.

(Hello, is anybody home?)

ごめんください.

Tanaka: Hai. Yā, Jōnzu-san. Yoku irasshaimashita. Dōzo oagari kudasai.

(Yes. Oh, Mr. Jones. Glad you could come. Please come in.)

はい. やあジョーンズさん. よくいらっしゃいました. どうぞおあがりください.

DIALOG (Cont.):

Jones: **Shitsurei shimasu.**
(Thank you. Lit: I do a rudeness.)
失礼します.

Tanaka: **Kochira e dōzo.** (This way, please.)
こちらへどうぞ.

(Giving *omiyage* to Tanaka)

Jones: **Tsumaranai mono desu ga .**
(This is nothing special, but . . . (please accept it).)
つまらない物ですが…

Tanaka: **Dōmo sumimasen.**
(Thank you.) `
どうもすみません.

(Offering dinner to Jones)

Tanaka: **Nanimo gozaimasen ga, dōzo goenryo naku.**
(I don't have anything (special), but please (have some) without hesitation.)
なにもございませんがどうぞご遠慮なく.

Jones: **Itadakimasu.**
(Thank you. Lit: I will receive (some).)
いただきます.

(Finishing dinner)

Jones: **Gochisōsama deshita.**
(It was very good.)

御馳走さまでした.

Tanaka: **Osomatsusama deshita.**
(Don't mention it. Lit: It was poor.)
お粗末さまでした.

(Leaving the house)

Jones: **Soro soro oitoma shimasu. Ojama shimashita.**
(I must be going. Thank you for everything.
Lit: I have been a bother to you.)
そろそろおいとまします. おじゃましました.

Tanaka: **Iie, mata dōzo.**
(Not at all, please (come) again.)
いいえ, またどうぞ.

Part Three
Living in Japan

30 At the Immigration Office

❶ **Nyū-ko-ku ka-n-ri ji-mu-sho** (Immigration Office)*
にゅうこくかんりじむしょ／入国管理事務所

② **sa-shō, bi-za** (visa)*
さしょう／査証，ビザ

❸ **ryo-ke-n, pa-su-pō-to** (passport)*
りょけん／旅券，パスポート

❹ **sa-i-nyū-ko-ku kyo-ka-shō** (re-entry permit)*
さいにゅうこくきょかしょう／再入国許可証

❺ **za-i-ryū ki-ka-n kō-shi-n** (extension of stay)*
ざいりゅうきかんこうしん／在留期間更新

⑥ **za-i-ryū shi-ka-ku** (status of residence)*
ざいりゅうしかく／在留資格　　　⌈residence)

⑦ **za-i-ryū shi-ka-ku he-n-kō** (change in status of
ざいりゅうしかくへんこう／在留資格変更

❽ **-kyo-ka shi-n-se-i-sho** (application for permission
きょかしんせいしょ／許可申請書　　⌊to...)*

⑨ **shu-sse-i to-do-ke** (registration of birth)
しゅっせいとどけ／出生届

⑩ **ho-shō-sho** (letter of guarantee)*
ほしょうしょ／保証書

⑪ **shō-me-i-sho** (certificate, note of authentica-
しょうめいしょ／証明書　　⌊tion)*

⑫ **za-i-sho-ku shō-me-i-sho** (letter of employment)*
ざいしょくしょうめいしょ／在職証明書 ⌈ment)*

⑬ **ge-n-se-n chō-shu-hyō** (tax withholding state-
げんせんちょうしゅうひょう／源泉徴収票

⑭ **ga-i-ji-n tō-ro-ku shō-me-i-sho**
(certificate of alien registration)*
がいじんとうろくしょうめいしょ／外人登録証明書

⑮ **ko-ku-se-ki** (nationality)
こくせき／国籍

⑯ **se-i-ne-n-ga-ppi** (date of birth)
せいねんがっぴ／生年月日

⑰ **ne-n-re-i** (age)
ねんれい／年令

⑱ **sho-ku-gyō** (occupation)
しょくぎょう／職業

⑲ **ho-n-se-ki** (permanent address)
ほんせき／本籍

⑳ **re-n-ra-ku-sa-ki** (contact address)
れんらくさき／連絡先

161

NOTES:

*❶ **Nyūkoku kanri jimusho:** Immigration regulations and procedures are too complicated to be fully explained here. Check with the Immigration Office for detailed information. The address of the Tokyo Immigration Office is:

3-20, Kōnan 3-chōme 　東京入国管理事務所
Minato-ku, Tokyo 　　東京都港区港南 3 丁目3–20
(Tel: 471-5111)

*❷ **sashō, biza:** Visas, if required, must be obtained before entering Japan. Tourist visas are usually easy to obtain, but other visas (commercial visas, student visas, etc.) are not issued if the applicant does not have the proper papers, often including a *hoshōsho* and a *shōmeisho* (see below).

*❸ **ryoken, pasupōto:** Tourists are legally required to carry their passports with them at all times during their stay in Japan.

*❹ **sainyūkoku kyokashō:** If you want to leave Japan and return again before your period of stay expires, you must first obtain a re-entry permit from an Immigration Office (unless your visa allows multiple re-entry already).

*❺ **zairyū kikan kōshin:** To extend your stay in Japan usually requires the same papers (*hoshōsho*, *shōmeisho*, etc.) as were necessary to obtain the original visa. Application must be made in person 10 days before your present stay expires.

*❻ **zairyū shikaku:** There are 16 different statuses which may be obtained if you qualify. Check with the Immigration Office in Japan or with the Japanese Embassy in your native country for details.

*❽ **-kyoka shinseisho:** The term *-kyoka shinseisho* is a suffix which refers to the application form necessary to complete the business indicated by the word it is attached to. For example, a *zairyū kikan kōshi-kyoka shinseisho* is an "application for permission to extend your stay in Japan."

*❿ **hoshōsho:** A letter of guarantee is required of foreigners who desire to stay in Japan for a long period of time. This letter should be prepared by a Japanese individual or organization (often an employer) who will promise to assist the foreigner if he has financial or other difficulties.

*⑪ **shōmeisho**: To get certain visas, a note of authentication is needed to verify your activities. If you are a student, for instance, you need one from your school to prove that you are actively engaged in study.

*⑫ **zaishoku shōmeisho**: If you are employed in Japan, you must obtain a letter of employment (showing the period of employment and how much money you will be earning) from your employer. If you are not employed, the Immigration Office may require some evidence of how you will support yourself during your stay.

*⑬ **gensen chōshūhyō**: The full term is **kyūyo shotoku no gensen chōshūhyō** (income tax withholding statement 給与所得の源泉徴収票). If you are employed in Japan and wish to extend your stay, you must present a copy of your income tax withholding statement along with the other necessary materials to the Immigration Office officials.

*⑭ **gaijin tōroku shōmeisho**: If you have one, you must carry your certificate of alien registration with you at all times. It is issued by the **kuyakusho** (ward office 区役所) or **shiyakusho** (city office 市役所) nearest your place of residence, and must be renewed periodically. Any change in address or other information included in the certificate must be officially changed at the issuing office.

ADDITIONAL WORDS:

Gaimushō (Foreign office 外務省)
shūnyū inshi (revenue stamps 収入印紙)
    You will need a thousand-yen revenue stamp to complete most business at the Immigration Office.
[Amerika] Taishikan ([American] Embassy [アメリカ] 大使館)

31 Buying or Renting a House or an Apartment

① **i-e** (house)
いえ／家

❷ **ə-pā-to, ma-n-sho-n** (apartment, flat)*
アパート，マンション

③ **ge-shu-ku** (boarding house, rooming house)
げしゅく／下宿

❹ **[yo-jō-ha-n] no he-ya** (a room the size of [four
[よじょうはん]のへや／[四畳半]の部屋 ⌐and a half *tatami* mats])*

⑤ **da-i-ni-n-gu ki-tchi-n** (combination dining-
ダイニングキッチン ⌐kitchen area)*

⑥ **su-i-se-n to-i-re** (flush toilet)*
すいせんトイレ／水洗トイレ

⑦ **to-chi** (land)
とち／土地

⑧ **tsu-bo** (unit of land measurement, 180 cm ×
つぼ／坪 ⌐180 cm)*

⑨ **ta-te-tsu-bo** (floor space)
たてつぼ／建坪

⑩ **shi-ki-chi** (lot, plot of ground)
しきち／敷地

❶❶ **ō-ya(-sa-n), ya-nu-shi** (landlord, landlady)
おおや(さん)／大家(さん)，やぬし／家主

⑫ **ji-nu-shi** (landholder)
じぬし／地主

❶❸ **fu-dō-sa-n-ya** (real-estate agency, real-estate
ふどうさんや／不動産屋 ⌐agent)

⑭ **shū-se-n-ryō** (commission)
しゅうせんりょう／周旋料

⑮ **ya-chi-n** (rent)
やちん／家賃

⑯ **shi-ki-ki-n** (deposit)*
しききん／敷金

⑰ **re-i-ki-n** (thank-you money)*
れいきん／礼金

⑱ **ke-n-ri-ki-n** (key money, premium)*
けんりきん／権利金

⑲ **a-ta-ma-ki-n** (down payment)
あたまきん／頭金

⑳ **[ni]-ne-n ke-i-ya-ku** ([two] year contract)
[にねん]けいやく／[二年]契約

NOTES:

*❷ apāto, manshon: The term *manshon* comes from the English word "mansion," but the meaning is different. To most Japanese, a *manshon* is more "luxurious" than an *apāto*, although both terms refer to the same things, apartments or apartment buildings.

*❹ yo-jōhan no heya: Japanese rooms are traditionally measured in terms of the number of *tatami* mats in them. Standard rooms contain **yo-jōhan** (4-1/2 mats 四畳半), **roku-jō** (6 mats 六畳), **hachi-jō** (8 mats 八畳), **jū-jō** (10 mats 十畳) and so on. Although there was a standard size for all *tatami* mats at one time (90 cm × 180 cm), modern construction practices have caused a reduction in the size of many of them, especially in apartments.

*❺ dainingu kitchin: A combination dining-kitchen area is common in many apartments and small houses. When such places are for rent, they are advertised as 2DK (meaning two rooms plus a dining-kitchen area), 3DK, etc.

*❻ suisen toire: A flush toilet should not be taken for granted in buying or renting a house; many houses have only a cesspool. Be sure to ask.

*❽ tsubo: The *tsubo* is used extensively in Japan to describe the area of a plot of ground or the floor space of a house. One *tsubo* is the size of two standard *tatami* mats.

*⑯ shikikin: When renting, a deposit is usually required, but it is refunded when you leave. The amount of the deposit is usually one or two months' rent, but varies according to the area where the apartment or house is located and the arrangements you make with the landlord.

*⑰ reikin: "Thank-you money" is a non-refundable payment made to the landlord before you move into an apartment or house which you rent. The *reikin* usually amounts to one or two months' rent and is paid in addition to the deposit and regular rent. Obviously, renting an apartment or house in Japan can be an expensive proposition.

166

*⓮ **kenrikin:** "Key money," like "thank-you money," is a non-refundable payment made to the landlord before you move into an apartment or house. Usually one or the other is required, not both.

USEFUL EXPRESSIONS:

1. **kau** (to buy) 買う
    Atarashii ie o kaitai n desu.
    (I want to buy a new house.)
    　　新しい家を買いたいんです.
2. **ni-kaidate** (two-storied) 二階建
    Go-heya gurai aru nikaidate no ie ga arimasu ka?
    (Do you have a two-storied house with about five rooms?)
    　　五部屋ぐらいある二階建の家がありますか.
3. **[Shibuya Eki] no chikaku ni ie o sagashite imasu.**
    (I am looking for a house in the vicinity of [Shibuya Station].)
    　　[渋谷駅] の近くに家をさがしています.
4. **kariru** (to rent) 借りる
    kagu-tsuki (furnished) 家具付
    Kagu-tsuki no heya o karitai n desu.
    (I want to rent a furnished room.)
    　　家具付の部屋を借りたいんです.
5. **basu-tsuki** (with a bath) バス付
    Sono apāto wa basu-tsuki desu ka?
    (Does that apartment have a bath?)
    　　そのアパートはバス付ですか.
6. **Suisen toire desu ka?**
    (Does it have a flush toilet?)
    　　水洗トイレですか.
7. **Yachin wa ikura desu ka?**
    (How much is the rent?)
    　　家賃はいくらですか.
8. **kōshin** (renewal) 更新
    Keiyaku no kōshin o shitai n desu ga.
    (I would like to renew the contract.)
    　　契約の更新をしたいんですが.

167

❶ **te-re-bi** (television)
テレビ

❷ **ra-ji-o** (radio)
ラジオ

❸ **su-te-re-o** (stereo)
ステレオ

❹ **re-i-zō-ko** (refrigerator)
れいぞうこ／冷蔵庫

❺ **se-n-pū-ki** (electric fan)
せんぷうき／扇風機

❻ **tō-su-tā** (toaster)
トースター

❼ **mi-ki-sā** (blender)*
ミキサー

⑧ **de-n-ki-ya(-sa-n)** (electrician)
でんきや(さん)／電気屋(さん)

⑨ **te-i-de-n** (power failure, power suspension)
ていでん／停電

⑩ **hyū-zu** (fuse)
ヒューズ

⑪ **tsu-ku-e** (desk)
つくえ／机

⑫ **ho-n-ba-ko** (bookcase)
ほんばこ／本箱

⑬ **te-n-jō** (ceiling)
てんじょう／天井

❹ **ka-be** (wall)
かべ／壁

❺ **yu-ka** (floor)
ゆか／床

⑯ **da-i-ku(-sa-n)** (carpenter)*
だいく(さん)／大工(さん)

❼ **na-ga-shi** (sink)
ながし／流し

⑱ **su-i-dō** (waterworks, plumbing)
すいどう／水道

⑲ **ga-su yu-wa-ka-shi-ki** (gas water heater)
ガスゆわかしき／ガス湯沸器

⑳ **se-ki-yu su-tō-bu** (kerosene heater)*
せきゆストーブ／石油ストーブ

NOTES:

*❼ **mikisā**: The term *mikisā* usually refers to a blender, but may also be used to refer to a mixer.

*⓰ **daiku(-san)**: Do-it-yourself carpenters are called **nichiyō daiku** (Sunday carpenters 日曜大工).

*⓴ **sekiyu sutōbu**: *Sekiyu* means kerosene, and it may be ordered from gas stations or **puropan gasu** (propane gas プロパンガス) dealers. Delivery is usually made in 18 liter cans.

ADDITIONAL WORDS:

gasu-ya(-san) (gas man ガス屋(さん))
penki-ya(-san) (house painter ペンキ屋(さん))
tatami-ya (*tatami* mat shop 畳屋)

The *tatami-ya* is the place where *tatami* mats are made, re-covered, or otherwise repaired. They will also turn the *tatami* mat cover over for you, a process which may be done once to renew the appeerence of the *tatami*.

tategu-ya (partition maker 建具屋)

The *tategu-ya* will make, re-paper, and repair your *shōji*, *fusuma*, or other doors. (See picture on page 156.)

USEFUL EXPRESSIONS:

1. **kowareru** (to be broken)
   こわれる
   [Terebi] ga kowaremashita.
   (The [television] is broken.)
   テレビがこわれました.
2. **naosu** (to fix) 直す
   Naoshi ni kite kudasai.
   (Please come to fix (it).)
   直しに来てください.

Sekiyu sutōbu (see ⓴)

170

3. **shūri** (repair) 修理
   Furui n desu ga, shūri dekimasu ka.
   (This is old, but can you fix it.)
   古いんですが修理できますか.

4. **Itsu dekimasu ka.**
   (When will it be ready?)
   いつできますか.

5. **[Denkiya-san] o yonde kudasai.**
   (Please call an [electrician] for me.)
   ［電気屋さん］を呼んでください.

6. **Hyūzu ga tobimashita.**
   (The fuse has burnt out.)
   ヒューズが飛びました.

7. **nurikaeru** (to repaint) 塗りかえる
   Daidokoro no kabe o nurikaetai n desu.
   (I want to repaint the walls of the kitchen.)
   台所の壁を塗りかえたいんです.

8. **harikaeru** (to re-paper, to re-cover)
   張りかえる
   Ie-jū no fusuma o harikaeru to, ikura gurai ni narimasu ka?
   (About how much will it cost if we re-paper the *fusuma* throughout the house?)
   家中のふすまを張りかえるといくらぐらいになりますか.

9. **omotegae o suru** (to re-cover)
   表がえをする
   Kono heya no tatami no omotegae o shite kudasai.
   (Please re-cover the *tatami* mats of this room.)
   この部屋の畳の表がえをしてください.

10. **moru** (to leak) 漏る
    Nagashi ga moru n desu ga, mite kudasai.
    (The sink leaks, so please look at it.)
    流しが漏るんですが見てください.

11. **nigoru** (to become muddy) 濁る
    Mizu ga nigotte imasu.
    (The water is dirty.)
    水が濁っています.

12. **Sekiyu o hito-kan motte kite kudasai.**
    (Please bring me one can of kerosene.)
    石油を一缶持って来てください.

33 Automobiles and Repairs

① **ku-ru-ma** (vehicle)
くるま／車

❷ **ji-dō-sha** (automobile)
じどうしゃ／自動車

③ **ka-shi-ji-dō-sha** (rent-a-car)*
かしじどうしゃ／貸自動車

❹ **to-ra-kku** (truck)
トラック

❺ **ō-to-ba-i** (motorcycle)
オートバイ

❻ **he-ru-me-tto** (helmet)
ヘルメット

⑦ **u-n-te-n me-n-kyo-shō** (driver's license)*
うんてんめんきょしょう／運転免許証

⑧ **dō-ro chi-zu** (road map)
どうろちず／道路地図

⑨ **ji-dō-sha shū-ri kō-jō** (car repair shop)
じどうしゃしゅうりこうじょう／自動車修理工場

⑩ **e-n-ji-n** (engine)
エンジン

⑪ **bu-rē-ki** (brake)
ブレーキ

❷ **ga-so-ri-n su-ta-n-do** (service station, gas station)
ガソリンスタンド

⑬ **ga-so-ri-n** (gasoline, petrol)
ガソリン

⑭ **o-i-ru** (oil)
オイル

⑮ **kū-ki** (air)
くうき／空気

❻ **pa-n-ku** (puncture, flat tire)
パンク

⑰ **kō-tsū ji-ko** (traffic accident)
こうつうじこ／交通事故

⑱ **ji-dō-sha ho-ke-n** (automobile insurance)
じどうしゃほけん／自動車保険

❶ **se-i-ge-n so-ku-do** (speed limit)
せいげんそくど／制限速度

❷ **kō-tsū ju-n-sa** (traffic policeman)
こうつうじゅんさ／交通巡査

NOTES:

*❼ **menkyoshō**: A Japanese driver's license may be obtained by showing your valid foreign license to the officials at a driver's licensing bureau. In addition, you must pass an eye test, pay the appropriate fees, and provide a few pictures of yourself. When you get your license, be sure to specify what you will use it for. Special fees are required for certain kinds of driving such as operating a motorcycle over 50 cc.

A **kokusai unten menkyoshō** (international driver's license 国際運転免許証) may also be obtained at the same office.

USEFUL EXPRESSIONS:

1. **Oiru mo mizu mo mite kudasai.**
   (Please check both the oil and the water.)
   オイルも水も見てください.

2. **Enjin ga chotto okashii n desu ga, shirabete kuremasen ka?**
   (The engine is (acting) a little strange, so could you please check it for me?)
   エンジンがちょっとおかしいんですが調べてくれませんか.

3. **koshō** (broken, out of order) 故障
   Batterii ga koshō shita rashii n desu. Mite kudasai.
   (The battery seems to be out of order. Please see how it is.)
   バッテリーが故障したらしいんです. 見てください.

4. **Panku shimashita. Naoshite kudasai.**
   ((The tire) is flat. Please fix it.)
   パンクしました. 直してください.

5. **Taiya ni kūki o irete kudasai.**
   (Please put air in the tires.)
   タイヤに空気を入れてください.

6. **rittoru** (liter) リットル
   Gasorin o jū-rittoru irete kudasai.
   (Please put in 10 liters of gasoline.)
   ガソリンを10リットル入れてください.

174

DIALOG:

(At a gas station)
Jones: **Mantan ni shite kudasai.**
(Please fill it up.)
満タンにしてください.
Attendant: **Regyurā desu ka? Sūpā desu ka?**
(Regular or Super?)
レギュラーですか, スーパーですか.
Jones: **Regyurā o onegai shimasu.**
(Give me regular.)
レギュラーをお願いします.

(Asking directions:)
Jones: **Tōkyō wa dotchi no hō desu ka?**
(Which direction is it to Tokyo?)
東京はどっちの方ですか.
Attendant: **Atchi desu.**
(It's that way.)
あっちです.
Jones: **Nanjikan gurai kakarimasu ka.**
(How long will it take (to get there)?)
何時間ぐらいかかりますか.
Attendant: **Hyaku-kiro desu kara, ni-jikan gurai deshō.**
(It will take about 2 hours, since it is 100 miles (from here).)
百キロですから二時間ぐらいでしょう.

AUTOMOBILE PARTS:

kuratchi (clutch クラッチ)
toransumisshon (transmission トランスミッション)
kyaburetā (carburetor キャブレター)
rajiētā (radiator ラジエーター)
mafurā (muffler マフラー)
hōn (horn ホーン)
waipā (windshield wipers ワイパー)
bakku mirā (rearview mirror バックミラー)

| 1 mile = 1.61 kilo | 50 mph = 80.5 kph |
| 0.62 mile = 1 kilo | 31.1 mph = 50 kph |

① **i-chi** (one)*
　　いち／一

② **ni** (two)
　　に／二

③ **sa-n** (three)
　　さん／三

④ **shi, yo-n** (four)
　　し，よん／四

⑤ **go** (five)
　　ご／五

⑥ **ro-ku** (six)
　　ろく／六

⑦ **shi-chi, na-na** (seven)
　　しち，なな／七

⑧ **ha-chi** (eight)
　　はち／八

⑨ **ku, kyū** (nine)
　　く，きゅう／九

⑩ **jū** (ten)
　　じゅう／十

① **a-ri-ga-tō go-za-i-ma-su** (thank you)*
　　ありがとうございます

② **wa-ta-ku-shi?** (me?)*
　　わたくし／私

⑬ **chi-ga-i-ma-su** (no)*
　　ちがいます／違います

⑭ **shi-tsu-re-i shi-ma-su** (excuse me)*
　　しつれいします／失礼します

⑮ **mi-chi o wa-ta-ri-ma-su** (I will cross the
　　みちをわたります／道を渡ります 　 ⌊street)*

⑯ **ki-te ku-da-sa-i** (please come here)*
　　きてください／来てください

⑰ **o-ka-ne** (money)*
　　おかね／お金

⑱ **do-ro-bō** (thief)*
　　どろぼう／泥棒

⑲ **o-to-ko** (man)*
　　おとこ／男

⑳ **o-n-na** (woman)*
　　おんな／女

NOTES:

GESTURES: Any langauge is composed of gestures as well as verbal symbols.   Below are some of the more common gestures used by the Japanese.

*❶ ichi: "Finger counting" in Japanese is done by closing the fingers of one hand, beginning with the thumb, then opening them again in reverse order up to 10. (Americans, however, will usually extend the fingers of both hands in counting to 10.)

*⓫ arigatō gozaimasu: The gesture being illustrated here is the famous Japanese bow.   Bowing is done not only when you say "thank you," but also when you greet someone (say "hello"), when you say "good-by," when you meet someone for the first time, and when you excuse yourself for making a blunder or causing someone inconvenience.   The best way to learn how to bow properly is to watch native Japanese and do as they do.

*⓬ watakushi?: When referring to himself with a gesture, the Japanese man will point to his nose. Women sometimes use the same gesture, but they will often point to their chest instead (which is more like the American gesture).

*⓭ chigaimasu: Literally, *chigaimasu* means "it is different."   The gesture (waving the hand in front of the face) is used whenever you wish to say "no," "I don't know," "I don't understand," "It's not me," "It's not mine," or to negate any request or question.

*⓮ shitsurei shimasu: When a man passess in front of someone, or between two or more people, he will use this gesture (a slight bow with his hand extended in a cutting-iike action) to excuse himself.   This gesture is not used so much by women.

*⓯ michi o watarimasu: This gesture (raising the hand to cross the street) is not used with the verbal expression *michi o watarimasu*. In fact, it is the only gesture mentioned here which does not have a verbal equivalent. Used mostly by children, this gesture indicates that the user is about to cross the street, and hopefully the drivers will stop.   Adults sometimes use a cross between this gesture and the one above (*shitsurei shimasu*) when crossing small ·streets especially those not marked with crosswalks.

*⑯ **kite kudasai:** Perhaps the first gesture to confuse Americans is the one used to call people, since it closely resembles the American gesture used to say good-by. The Japanese gesture for good-by is an open hand, palm toward the one you are waving to, waved left and right. These gestures are used between good friends, and never to a superior.

*⑰ **okane:** This gesture is used to indicate something like "I have money," or "I need money," depending on the context of the conversation. Recently, it has come to mean "OK" in the American sense, too.

*⑱ **dorobō:** This gesture (looking something like the repeated squeezing of a trigger) is used when referring to a thief. Obviously, there is not much occasion to use this gesture, but it appears from time to time.

*⑲ **otoko:** This gesture (the thumb extended) is used to indicate a man. Used by men in rather informal situations, it is not commonly used in daily conversation and is rarely found in formal contexts.

*⑳ **onna:** This gesture (the little finger extended) is used exclusively by men in very informal situations to inquire if someone has a girl friend or wife.

ADDITIONAL WORDS:

gomasuri (flattery, apple polishing 胡麻すり)

When you want to "accuse" someone of flattering you, rotate your closed hand in a clockwise direction in front of your stomach and in a horizontal plane. The bigger the circle, the bigger the flattery you are "accusing" the other person of. Such an "accusation" is made under friendly rather than serious circumstances.

baka (fool 馬鹿)

If you want to say that someone is a fool, you move your hand in a circular motion above your ear. After two or so rotations, open your hand with the fingers pointing up and stop the motion. Be careful of this gesture and the term *baka* as they are dynamite if used in the wrong situation. Although known by every elementary school child, the word *baka* is a harsh word in certain situations.

COUNTERS:

-nin (people - 人)

hitori	一人	one person
futari	二人	two people
san-nin	三人	three people
yo-nin	四人	four people

-satsu (bound objects 一冊)

This counter is used for books, magazines, etc.

issatsu	一冊	one bound object
ni-satsu	二冊	two bound objects
san-satsu	三冊	three bound objects

-ken (houses 一軒)

ikken	一軒	one house
ni-ken	二軒	two houses
san-gen	三軒	three houses

-ban (number 一番)

ichi-ban	一番	number one
ni-ban	二番	number two
san-ban	三番	number three

See also the counters **-mai** (page 21) and **-hon** (page 46).

San-satsu (Three books)   Ni-ken (Two houses)

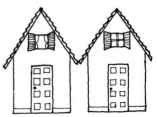

COUNTING:

ichi	一	hitotsu	一つ	1
ni	二	futatsu	二つ	2
san	三	mittsu	三つ	3
yon, shi	四	yottsu	四つ	4
go	五	itsutsu	五つ	5
roku	六	muttsu	六つ	6
shichi, nana	七	nanatsu	七つ	7
hachi	八	yattsu	八つ	8
ku, kyū	九	kokonotsu	九つ	9
jū	十	tō	十	10

jū-ichi	十一	11
jū-ni	十二	12
jū-san	十三	13
ni-jū	二十	20
ni-jū-ichi	二十一	21
san-jū	三十	30
yon-jū	四十	40
hyaku	百	100
ni-hyaku	二百	200
san-byaku	三百	300
yon-hyaku	四百	400
go-hyaku	五百	500
roppyaku	六百	600
nana-hyaku	七百	700
happyaku	八百	800
kyū-hyaku	九百	900
sen	千	1,000
ni-sen	二千	2,000
san-zen	三千	3,000
hassen	八千	8,000
kyūsen	九千	9,000
ichi-man	一万	10,000
ni-man	二万	20,000
jū-man	十万	100,000
hyaku-man	百万	1,000,000
sen-man	千万	10,000,000
ichi-oku	一億	100,000,000

INDEX

Japanese:

The following Japanese index includes all the words found in the basic vocabulary lists and all of the words introduced separately on the subsequent pages of each section. All numbers are page numbers; "n" means that a note of explanation will be found on that page.

I

188

U

English:

The following English index includes only the words which are easy to translate into English and which might be placed in different sections of this book. Words which are rather technical in nature or obviously relate to a particular section of the book may be found by consulting the appropriate section. For instance, the word for a "*sumō* wrestler" will be found in section 21, which is about *sumō*; words for Japanese clothing will be found by consulting section 27, which is about Japanese apparel. See the inside of the front and back covers for other sections which deal with such technical or "untranslatable words." In this index, all numbers are page numbers; "n" means that a note of explanation will be found on that page.

196

200

SUBJECT INDEX

(Numbers refer to SECTIONS of the book)